100 YEARS
of Baseball on
ST. PETERSBURG'S WATERFRONT

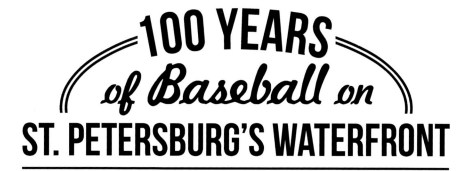

100 YEARS
of Baseball on
ST. PETERSBURG'S WATERFRONT

HOW THE GAME HELPED SHAPE A CITY

RICK VAUGHN
FOREWORD BY TIM KURKJIAN

THE
History
PRESS

Published by The History Press
Charleston, SC
www.historypress.com

Front cover, top left: courtesy of the Library of Congress; *top center*: courtesy of St. Petersburg Museum of History; *top right*: courtesy of the Boston Public Library, Leslie Jones Collection; *bottom*: courtesy of Skip Milos.
Back cover, top left: CardCow.com, public domain; *top right*: CardCow.com, public domain; *bottom*: courtesy of St. Petersburg Museum of History.

First published 2022

Manufactured in the United States

ISBN 9781467152860

Library of Congress Control Number: 2022936211

It was in our backyard where my dad gifted me his love for the game. He would pull the family Olds into the driveway at the end of a long day of work and often find me throwing a tennis ball against the side of the house. All it took was, "Hey, Dad…?" and, unfailingly, he would duck into the house to kiss my mom, grab the big Spalding catcher's mitt and a grass-stained baseball and head down the side-door steps to the yard, where our homemade pitching rubber and home plate were planted a Little League regulation forty-six feet apart. Dinner would be temporarily delayed.

Still in his work clothes, he would squat down, hold up that glove and give me a target just below his shirt pocket with the name Bill sewn above it. My dad was tall, and when he crouched down behind that plywood plate, he was a big target. I felt I could hit that glove wherever he held it with every pitch. It was at those times that the world was perfect; my first experiences of being in "the zone," and I was in there with my dad. And it was fueled, not by a father's insistence, but simply by our shared love for the game.

Much later, when I was at the local college on a baseball scholarship, he got away from work as often as he could to see me pitch, but I was too immature to understand how important those games were to him. The greatest, most humble man I ever met dropped out of high school his senior year to enlist in the U.S. Navy as World War II broke out. Just before fall ball my sophomore year, he died suddenly. This book is dedicated to him and to my mom, who made sure I never missed a practice or a game, and to the three women in my life who sacrificed much so that I could live out a fantasy life of working in Major League Baseball for thirty years. I'm referring to the beautiful Sue, mi amor, and my bench coach for forty-two years; and my daughters, Elissa, wonderful mother to our grandson, Mason; and Dr. Amanda Vaughn, whose creative spirit and curiosity are unmatched. Love you guys.

CONTENTS

FOREWORD

The first spring training game I ever attended was in 1974, my senior year in high school. Our family had traveled from Maryland to Florida to watch my oldest brother, Andy, a star catcher at Catholic University, play games at the Phillies' complex in Clearwater. My dad, who loved baseball, took my mom and my two brothers to a spring training game between the Cardinals and Mets. My dad, who had such a great feel for the game, specifically chose one ballpark for our first game because he had been there, and he understood its stature and significance. The Cardinals' Ted Simmons, a favorite, hit a homer to right field. It was unforgettable, a perfect day, because it happened at Al Lang Field.

I have since seen a spring training game in well over fifty ballparks, and Al Lang Field in St. Petersburg is still my favorite, still the best. And my dear friend Rick Vaughn, who, like my dad, has a great love and feel for the best game in the world, brings Al Lang Field and its predecessor, Waterfront Park, back to life one hundred years after its birth in this beautifully written and meticulously reported book. It will capture the imagination of anyone who believes spring training is paradise, the best time of the year. It will warm the hearts of anyone who has sat in the sunshine on a lazy afternoon in March in Florida or Arizona to watch big leaguers ready for 162.

I have watched dozens of spring training games at Al Lang Field, I thought I knew it well. But until I read this book, I had no idea of the richness of its history. I learned that 193 Hall of Famers played there, including Babe Ruth, Lou Gehrig, Ted Williams, Stan Musial, Joe DiMaggio, Willie

Mays, Hank Aaron, Mickey Mantle and Sandy Koufax, not to mention actor Jimmy Stewart and the fictional pitcher Sidd Finch. I learned that twenty-three championship seasons began there, many by the Yankees and Cardinals, perhaps the two most decorated franchises in baseball history, who combined for nearly seventy spring trainings in that beautiful park on the St. Pete waterfront. Rick expertly weaves many nuggets, facts and delightful stories through this fascinating history lesson.

It is a story that really has never been fully told. And it is not exclusively about baseball; it's about how a city developed itself around a ballpark, the tourism it created and the opportunities it brought to so many. It is about civil rights, about Jackie Robinson, about activism. Sadly, a baseball game has not been played at Al Lang Field in fourteen years, but this is not a story that should be forgotten. As development continues relentlessly throughout St. Petersburg, a good deal of it started with a ballpark built on the water in 1921.

Yes, Al Lang Field was only a spring training ballpark, but that doesn't detract from its importance and value. Spring training is a critical time for teams and players. It is often where a winning atmosphere is first sculpted, where fundametals are stressed, where stars are discovered and disappear. The wins and losses, and the statistics, might seem not to matter, but they do. Some of my best learning experiences as a writer came in spring training.

Rick Vaughn was the public relations director for the Baltimore Orioles during the four years (1986–89) I covered the team as the beat guy for the *Baltimore Sun*. He was as good a PR professional as there has ever been, in part because I have never met a PR guy who understands baseball, the competition of the game, better than Rick. On the beat, we called him Mr. Rickey—I still do on first reference—as a tribute to one of the most important people in baseball history, Branch Rickey. Writer Jim Henneman calls Rick "Arky," after Arky Vaughan, a Hall of Fame shortstop who played games at Al Lang Field.

The reason Rick has such a ferocious love for the game is because he played it. He was a star pitcher at George Mason University in Fairfax, Virginia. He threw *hard*. When the writers and Oriole staffers played our silly media game once a year at Memorial Stadium and Oriole Park at Camden Yards, Rick always pitched, because he knew what he was doing—as always, without ego. We are all thankful that he didn't throw as hard as he could, or it would have been a quick game. No one would have put the ball in play.

I thought I knew Mr. Rickey really well, but I must say, I didn't know he was such a gifted writer. No PR man wrote the pregame notes better than

Rick, but they didn't require great prose or intricate storytelling. They did require great research, and no PR guy has recognized an interesting note, a cogent fact and a compelling story better than Rick. I'm sure he spent countless hours in the library scouring old newspaper clippings, vintage photos and microfilm for the best of the best of the beautiful and historic Al Lang Field.

I will not tell of any of those stories here.

Read on.

You'll learn something on every page. This book will take you back in time. And it will warm your heart like a spring training game at Al Lang Field.

—Tim Kurkjian

INTRODUCTION

L ike the ballparks that followed, St. Petersburg's public waterfront, created in 1910, wasn't an easy birth. The owner of a small power plant where the St. Petersburg Yacht Club is now located wanted to develop the city's shoreline into a sprawling commercial harbor. But according to the Poynter Institute's Politifact, *St. Petersburg Times* editor William Straub and real estate developer C. Perry Snell, champions of the City Beautiful movement, preferred a public space that could be enjoyed by all. The two men pooled their resources to covertly buy parcels of what was then a commercial shoreline in order to thwart plans for industrialization. Straub and Snell deeded their land, paid for with their own money, to the city as public parkland. The plan was met with some derision by many St. Petersburg taxpayers.

Historian and author Raymond Arsenault Raymond Arsenault told Politifact: "It was a small city. (Straub and Snell) wanted to keep as much waterfront as pristine as possible. They had a vision of a resort city, which was unusual. There were smaller towns with parks like that, but the idea of a city growing on tourism was a pretty novel idea."

It became, as the *St. Petersburg Times* described it in 1919, the city's "front yard…everybody's lawn."

In his book *The Making of St. Petersburg*, historian Will Michaels proclaimed, "One thing is certain, baseball, like the waterfront parks, have been a big part of St. Petersburg's history and its sense of place."

Amen.

St. Petersburg's waterfront, circa 1955. *Courtesy of St. Petersburg Museum of History.*

WHILE IT IS TRUE that spring training baseball was first held in St. Petersburg in 1914 on a long-lost field somewhere near Coffee Pot Bayou, the city's roots in the great game are buried elsewhere. It was later on the waterfront grounds between First Street and First Avenue that we saw 193 Hall of Famers play or manage, including members of the first induction class and the latest. Of these, 28 appeared in the spring of 1968 alone; 12 others played in one game in 1933. We witnessed hundreds of games played by the two most successful teams in major league history, the Yankees and Cardinals, on their way to 27 and 11 World Series titles, respectively. It was there where 23 World Series champions and 37 league champions began their seasons, the Gashouse Gang, Murderer's Row, the Miracle Mets and our own 2008 American League champion Rays among them. There were eighteen clashes between defending league champions. Three teams played their inaugural games there.

And it all started one hundred years ago, when the Boston Braves became the first of seven teams to train there on diamonds with overlapping footprints. Whether it was Waterfront Park or Al Lang Field, Al Lang

Stadium or Florida Power/Progress Energy Park at Al Lang Field, major leaguers played on the hallowed bayside grounds for nearly ninety springs. The last major league game played there was March 28, 2008, ending a run that saw the Braves, Yankees, Cardinals, Giants, Mets, Orioles and Rays call it home.

"You could make the case that more great players played there than on any field in history," ten-time All-Star and Tampa native Steve Garvey told me. Even Jimmy Stewart starred there, and not just the Jimmy Stewart who was one of baseball's first super utility guys in the 1960s and '70s, but *the* Jimmy Stewart, who could be seen in more than eighty films and wore a Cardinals uniform in *Strategic Air Command*, filmed in part at Al Lang in 1955.

And yet, it may have been an aging, journeyman infielder trying to make a comeback, a phenom pitcher who never threw a pitch and a beloved hot dog vendor who put the most eyes on the waterfront wonderland. And football, always football.

In March 1979, forty-one-year-old infielder Chico Esquela, a fictional character played by comedian Garrett Morris on NBC's *Saturday Night Live*, taped a skit at Al Lang with Bill Murray before a Mets game. Twenty-five million people saw it. Concluding possibly the greatest April Fools' joke of all time, the Mets announced at a home plate ceremony that their otherworldly rookie hurler Hayden "Sidd" Finch was giving up baseball. The fictitious Finch (played by Joe Berton, a junior high art instructor from Oak Park, Illinois), was a creation of George Plimpton and *Sports Illustrated*. Their fourteen-page story about a world-traveling, French horn–playing Harvard alum with a 168-mile-per-hour fastball went viral in the spring of 1985, twenty years before Twitter.

One year later, Al Lang Stadium's beloved singing hot dog vendor, Tommy Walton, appeared on *The Tonight Show* with Johnny Carson. At the time, Carson was attracting somewhere around ten million viewers a night. And in 1958 and 1959, Al Lang Field hosted the Holiday Bowl college football games, televised to fifteen million viewers by CBS-TV.

It may not have been exactly what the baseball mastermind and two-time mayor Al Lang envisioned when he secured a downtown ballpark with a ninety-nine-year lease and a water view for a minor league club in 1921. In fact, it became more.

Starting in 1958, when the Florida Winter Instructional League began, Al Lang Field / Stadium annually hosted more than 150 professional baseball games: Grapefruit League teams in the spring, minor league baseball in the summer and instructional league games in the fall and winter—all of it against a backdrop worthy of a Guy Harvey painting.

Charles Fountain described Waterfront Park in his book *Under the March Sun*: "Its most remarkable feature—on Opening Day in 1922 and for eight decades that followed—was its setting. Just beyond the outfield grass were the sparkling waters of Tampa Bay." And in its last year as a major league spring site, the *New York Times'* George Vecsey wrote, "The most delightful place on the planet to watch an exhibition is St. Petersburg alongside the rippling waters of Tampa Bay."

A paradox. That was how Joe Magrane, the National League's 1988 ERA (earned run average) leader and former Rays television analyst, described it not long ago: "Standing on the mound in 1987, my Cardinals debut against the World Champion Mets and we're getting ready to start. We're throwing the ball around the infield and [Cardinals third baseman] Terry Pendleton is throwing it to me and I almost drop it because at the same time I'm looking out at the marina. I'm thinking in three innings I could be out there in a boat drinking a beer. It was like being in the middle of a theme park. I loved it."

Imagine how joyous Lang and the city's first publicity director John Lodwick would have been had they been around on March 16, 1968, when the Cardinals' future Hall of Famer Orlando Cepeda hit a two-run home run in an exciting 5–4 win over the Mets and Tom Seaver while a pyramid of water-skiers from the local boat show skipped along the bay behind them. No staging was needed for that travel poster.

Wrote longtime *Minneapolis Star Tribune* columnist Patrick Reusse recently: "An afternoon at Al Lang was one of the reasons that, as I stated years ago, 'Spring training is the greatest invention in the history of American sports writing.'"

Just before the last Grapefruit League game was played there on March 28, 2008, Tampa Bay Rays manager Joe Maddon said this about Al Lang Stadium: "Believe me, you can't find a better setting for a spring training baseball game to be played. For those that never had a chance to encounter it, it's too bad because this truly is the essence of spring training."

Maddon's connection with this field of dreams is deep-rooted. As a freshman pitcher-catcher in 1973, his Lafayette College team escaped Pennsylvania's cold March spring for a series of games at the University of Tampa. Finding himself free one evening, he snuck away from the group and hitchhiked in the back of a pickup truck across the bay to watch the Cardinals play the Mets at Al Lang. "Had to be by myself. I didn't want anyone messing this up for me," recalled the current skipper of the Los Angeles Angels and three-time Manager of the Year. "It was magical. I wanted to totally enjoy the moment. I could not believe I was watching an actual Cardinal spring training baseball game versus the Mets in St. Petersburg. For me it was about Al Lang and getting that opportunity."

It was the same way for the game's umpires. "It was the epitome of working a spring game," said veteran major league umpire Richie Garcia, who began his career there in the Florida State League in 1970. "For a young umpire, working a spring training game at Al Lang, especially a night game, was like Yankee Stadium. It was the only game in town, and at night you saw all the baseball people there."

Spring training box scores have the lifespan of a mayfly, dissolving before the players reach the postgame showers. But our own joyful memories and those handed down from parents and grandparents remain.

We heard about the most recognizable athlete on the planet carousing our Prohibition-proof bars and our outfield. Babe Ruth's fun was not limited to his oft-repeated nighttime shenanigans; he playfully wore fake whiskers during a Yankees game on the waterfront against the bearded House of David nine. Between innings of a 4–1 loss to the Reds, he was given a baby alligator by the local Order of Elks. He promptly unleashed the creature upon the Yankees' home bench. Primarily because of the cavernous nature of the park, some curious ground rules and the number of days he missed while squabbling over his contract with Yankees owner Colonel Jacob Ruppert, Ruth hit only 13 home runs in his eleven springs at Waterfront Park. But his last home run there in 1934 is not forgotten in local baseball circles. Legend has it that the right-field blast hit the second-floor porch of the seventy-eight-room West Coast Inn, at the time the spring headquarters of the Boston Braves. Demolished in 1967 at the site now occupied by the St. Pete Hilton across First Street South, the hotel was more than six hundred feet from home plate, which at that time was located in what is now the parking lot of the soccer pitch that is now Al Lang.

No player, not even Ruth, brought crowds to the waterfront like Jackie Robinson. In St. Petersburg's long spring training history, just two games drew more than eight thousand fans, both featuring Robinson and the Brooklyn Dodgers. Only nineteen spring games ever drew seven thousand or more. In Jackie's seven games there, the *average* crowd was 7,433. And Jackie responded in kind, batting .346 with a home run.

Willie Mays's first spring in St. Petersburg was the last of his twenty-three-year career. Troubled by a sore right knee that would hasten his retirement

Babe Ruth at the Yankees' practice facility at Crescent Lake Park. *Courtesy of the Library of Congress.*

that year, Mays was able to play in only five games at Al Lang, but true to form, he homered in three of them.

Joe DiMaggio hit his first 2 home runs in a Yankees uniform in our town. We saw him get 10 hits in his first 13 at bats at Waterfront Park in 1936 before a freak training-room accident sidelined him for the rest of his rookie Grapefruit League season. Three years later, it was St. Pete fans who were the first to see what was perhaps the Yankees' greatest outfield ever—DiMaggio, Tommy Henrich and Charlie Keller—start together for the first time in a 7–6 loss to the Cardinals. In 1941, the trio would become major league's first outfield to hit 30 home runs each. It is still the only Yankee outfield to do it. And no one celebrated the end of World War II like DiMaggio, who hit 15 home runs in the spring of 1946, including 7 in twelve games during Waterfront Park's last season.

In a win over the Braves in 1930, Yankees third baseman Ben Chapman hit what might have been baseball's first "splash" home run, into Tampa Bay, seventy years before they became the rage at San Francisco's AT&T Park.

For nineteen springs, we witnessed the man that Commissioner Ford Frick called "baseball's perfect warrior, baseball's perfect knight," Stan Musial, become one of our own. He played for seven different managers, before seven different city mayors and to the delight of nearly one million waterfront admirers. Stan played in more than two hundred Grapefruit League games there and hit 19 home runs, both more than any other player. One of those home runs broke the bulbs in a right-field light tower some 385 feet from home plate, sending glass down on First Street, not unlike Roy Hobbs's walk-off home run in Barry Levinson's 1984 hit movie *The Natural.*

Mickey Mantle, who could have easily stood in for Robert Redford for the film's action scenes, gave us a preview of his 1956 Triple Crown season when he crushed 5 home runs out of Al Lang that spring and a few doubles and triples. All of the home runs went more than 400 feet, and 2 of them landed in Tampa Bay's waters.

Hall of Famers Stan Musial (*left*) and Mickey Mantle before the spring opener at Al Lang on March 9, 1958. The two shared the ballpark for ten seasons. *AP photo.*

We smiled at what had to be an irritated Ted Williams in 1940 as he sprinted around the bases to avoid being tagged out to score the only run of the game after he slugged a 440-foot drive off a palm tree in the field of play in center field at Waterfront Park.

In one week in 1960, we saw two future Hall of Fame Dodger teammates, twenty-four-year-old Sandy Koufax and twenty-three-year-old Don Drysdale, earn wins over the Cardinals and Yankees under beautiful St. Pete skies.

We saw the waterfront's winningest warrior, a fearless young right-hander named Bob Gibson, not even on the roster, beat that season's world champions, the Dodgers. It was the first of 22 wins he would record at Al Lang, more than any other pitcher. Soon after came fellow future Hall of Famer Tom Seaver, who shared the waterfront mound with Gibson for nine springs. The most famous Met made 30 career starts there and only three times did he allow more than 2 earned runs.

Always a visitor, Hank Aaron hit 6 home runs in only thirteen games at Al Lang. As a twenty-year-old rookie, his career was jump-started there when the Braves' incumbent left fielder, Bobby Thomson, broke his ankle on a slide into second base. "Hammerin' Hank" even made a rare start at third base in St. Pete when his manager, Birdie Tebbetts, forgot he didn't bring another future Hall of Famer, Eddie Mathews, on the trip from Bradenton.

We saw eight-time National League batting champion Tony Gwynn win a one-time, made-for-TV event called the Big League Baseball Decathlon Challenge in his only appearance at Al Lang. In the 1964 spring home opener, we were delighted when the Cardinals opened with the same infield that started the previous All-Star game: first baseman Bill White, second baseman Julian Javier, shortstop Dick Groat and third baseman Ken Boyer. In 1924, the waterfront was the site of the unlikeliest of events: the 100-loss Boston Braves won a 1–0 game over the defending National League champion New York Giants, which boasted a lineup that featured seven future Hall of Famers.

On March 28, 1959, we welcomed two future presidents. In the afternoon, Cardinals' outfielder–first baseman, Bill White, acquired from the Giants just four days before, homered in his Al Lang debut. In the evening, presidential hopeful John F. Kennedy spoke there for the first time, urging a crowd of about one thousand to utilize the talents of its senior citizens. Kennedy was elected the thirty-fifth president of the United States in 1961, and White was voted the thirteenth president of the National League in 1989.

And there was much, much more. There were the leg kicks of a pair of Giants: Juan Marichal on the mound and Mel Ott at the plate. We saw

Seven members of the American League All-Star team of 1937. They all played at St. Pete. *From left to right*: Lou Gehrig, Joe Cronin, Bill Dickey, Joe DiMaggio, Charley Gehringer, Jimmie Foxx and Hank Greenberg. *Courtesy of the Library of Congress.*

Bob Uecker throw Roberto Clemente out at second base. (Oh, yes, we did.) Joe Torre, who wore a home uniform at Al Lang for eighteen seasons as a manager and a player, hit 3 home runs in one game and 6 in one spring prior to his 1971 Most Valuable Player season. We gasped at Ozzie Smith's backflips. We were shocked when the expansion Mets walked it off against the Yankees in the first-ever game between the two. In the Cardinals' 9–2 win over the Mets on March 23, 1973, there were three brothers—Jose, Hector and Tommy Cruz—filling the outfield and the first three spots in the batting order for the only time in major league history. Maybe our grandfathers or great-grandfathers saw Tris Speaker, among the first eight players elected to the Hall of Fame, smack a line-drive home run *under* the fence in his first at bat at Waterfront Park. There was a game in 1960 when the Cardinals' journeyman infielder Daryl Spencer hit 3 home runs, drew 2 walks, scored 5 runs and drove in 5 to produce the rarely seen 3-5-3-5 box score line in a win over the Yankees.

On March 17, 1988, another oddity played out on the waterfront when the Astros' battery featured a pair of future Hall of Famers: forty-one-year-old Nolan Ryan, already baseball's all-time strikeout leader, and his twenty-two-year-old rookie catcher, Craig Biggio. There was local ambassador Don Zimmer, a forever resident of the area, who wore six different uniforms on the waterfront, including that of the Washington Senators' winter instructional league team as he worked to improve his catching skills at the unheard-of age of thirty-three! We "heard" Walter Johnson's fastball on an April day in 1924. And it was in March 1992 at Al Lang that heartthrobs Kevin Costner and Tom Selleck couldn't get to first base on the same night. (Both were hitless in the Legends of Baseball Classic, part of a series of old-timer games played there for nearly fifty years). It was also the only place where baseball's two ironmen each called home.

It was one of those men with whom we agonized firsthand during the spring of 1939. While baseball fans across the country were reading about Lou Gehrig's mysterious spring slump from the accounts of dozens of newspapers with St. Petersburg datelines, those filling the stands at Waterfront Park were seeing it live, already asking themselves, "What is wrong with the Iron Horse?" "He was not always a great spring training hitter," they may have told themselves. "But this is different."

"Lou was sluggish and inept all through spring training, but he never stopped trying," wrote longtime sportswriter Fred Lieb who, because of their shared German heritage, had developed a friendship with Gehrig. In back-to-back home games against the Cardinals, Gehrig went 0-for-4 in a 7–6 loss and then 0-for-5 while his teammates racked up 17 hits in a 12–7 triumph. After the first game, Lieb wrote: "He insisted 'I've got to train more.' Sure enough he was out at Miller Huggins Field the next morning before any of the rookies and dragged his aching, ailing body through a long workout before the afternoon game." On March 27, in what would be Lou's last game at Waterfront Park, the Yankees fell to the Dodgers, 3–2. Gehrig went 1-for-3 and singled in his last at bat, unbelievably one of only four hits he got against major league pitching on the waterfront all spring. All were singles. He was out of the lineup on May 2 and died from ALS two years later.

Against a background often duplicated on postcards, our elders saw the fiery Ty Cobb ejected from his only game in St. Petersburg and, later, future Hall of Fame shortstop Rabbit Maranville break his left leg in a home-plate collision so horrific that the game was not resumed. It ranked as perhaps the worst injury ever on the waterfront until Devil Rays southpaw Tony Saunders broke the humerus bone in his left arm *for the second time* while throwing a pitch during a rehab start in a minor league game on a rainy evening sixty-six years later.

Almost as gruesome was Don Larsen's first start after his perfect game for the Yankees in Game 5 of the 1956 World Series. He lost, 20–6, at Al Lang. Mantle and Roger Maris gave no hint of the historic race they were about to begin in 1961 when the two combined to hit only 1 home run at home that spring. Yankees owner George Steinbrenner got into the act when he found a Cardinals fan in his Al Lang seat in a 1981 game. Just like that, it was fourteen years before the Yankees returned to play the Cards on the waterfront, something they had done 135 times in the previous fifty-seven seasons

The three bayside ballparks were not without their bizarre moments, and who else but the irrepressible Casey Stengel should top the list? As the sixty-five-year-old manager of the Yankees, Stengel was arrested and jailed for assaulting a photographer near the home dugout and then, two days later on the same field, given the key to the city as part of a pregame presentation celebrating the Yankees' thirtieth anniversary in St. Petersburg. There was the game against the Yankees in 1953 when the Braves began the contest representing Boston and finished it as Milwaukee's team after league owners approved the franchise's move at a midgame meeting at the Vinoy Hotel less than a mile away. In the pre–Skyway Bridge era, we saw the Yankees and Red Sox play seventeen innings, only to have the game halted so the Red Sox could catch the Bee Line Ferry across Tampa Bay to Sarasota. And, on March 19, 1926, Ruth crashed 2 long doubles, the affable Gehrig was ejected from the game and an airplane crashed in Tampa Bay behind the third-base grandstand. A triple steal? We saw the Tigers pull one off against Casey Stengel's Yankees with Hall of Famer George Kell on the front end. How about another Hall of Famer, Andre Dawson, hitting into three bases-loaded double plays, two against Doc Gooden, in the same game? We witnessed Joe Louis box, the Harlem Globetrotters dribble (even if it was on rain-soaked hardwood), the Flying Wallendas walk high over Al Lang's infield without a net and sitting President George H.W. Bush jog around its warning track.

And where else could you go to have your senses assaulted by the combination of two male streakers and the stench from the latest Red Tide outbreak before receiving relief from, of all sources, a Mets victory. Baseball on the waterfront also had its own sped-up rules. "The spring games there went fast," explained Magrane, "because if a game wasn't finished by about 4 o'clock all of the seagulls came in—like thousands of them—and they were [relieving themselves] all over the place. The guys who needed to get their work in late in the game needed to hurry, because it had a chance to look like a scene from Hitchcock's *The Birds*."

While it was all special, it was also, after all, spring training. What else explains the Yankees and Reds walking 25 batters in a ten-inning game? Or the Dodgers and Mets having nine runners thrown out on the bases in a messy Dodgers win in 1965? Or Joe Pignatano stealing third base with two outs in the ninth inning and his team trailing by two runs, only to find a Dodger teammate already there? Or the Senators' pitching staff walking 16 batters in nine innings and winning when the Cardinals left 15 men on base? Or the Pirates' Steve Blass's pitching line in a 5–4 loss to the Cardinals: four innings pitched, 0 hits, 5 runs, 9 walks, 2 strikeouts and 1 hit batter? Or, in their third game as first-time defending world champions, the Amazin' Mets making 8 errors in a 12–3 loss to the Phillies, who themselves allowed 6 unearned runs with two outs in the ninth in an 8–7 walk-off loss to the Cardinals in 1968?

Primarily through the efforts of the Sunshine City's greatest advocate, Al Lang, others were able to read about it all through the lenses of some of the greatest sportswriters of their day. Nearly every winner of the Baseball Writers Association of America's (BBWAA) Annual Career Excellence Award—some seventy-two sportswriters—covered a game on the waterfront. The BBWAA, so taken with Lang, made him an honorary member of their select group. It might have even been possible that the practice of feeding the media in the press box originated at the park that bore Lang's name. While on the hunt for another pitcher, Indians owner Bill Veeck attended a Yankees-Cardinals game in 1948. Coatless and tieless, Veeck decided to sit with the writers atop the roof of the new ballpark. The one-of-a-kind baseball icon asked for a Coke and a sandwich and was told that that was not standard operating procedure at the Al Lang press box. Veeck, with his artificial leg, clambered down the stairs and returned with fifty hot dogs, fifty ice-cream containers and fifty bottles of Coke to share with the members of the fourth estate.

Hall of Fame broadcasters routinely passed through the waterfront, but 1951 saw greats Harry Caray, Ernie Harwell and Russ Hodges spend all spring there broadcasting games of the Giants and Cardinals. And at least one broadcasting career was born at Al Lang. Former Cy Young Award winner Rick Sutcliffe, who has been a part of ESPN's baseball coverage for twenty-four years, was pitching for the Orioles in 1992 and 1993 when they trained on the waterfront. Under normal circumstances, starting pitchers aren't required to stay for spring games on days they are not pitching, but manager Johnny Oates asked the veteran ace to stick around to critique a pair of prized number-one draft picks, Mike Mussina and Ben McDonald,

Grantland Rice was one of many great sportswriters to cover games on the waterfront. *Courtesy of the Library of Congress.*

during their spring starts. Sutcliffe would do so from the stands until, one day, another Hall of Fame broadcaster, the O's Jon Miller, invited him up to Al Lang's home radio booth. It quickly became Sutcliffe's routine, and he immediately discovered how easy describing a game came to him. "That's where it all started for me, right there," Sutcliffe told me. "When I first started interviewing for jobs, I was told I was a natural. It was at Al Lang when I first realized that. I knew then that was what I wanted to do when I was done pitching."

While none of what went on at the waterfront counted for anything at all in baseball's holy record books, it created some of the game's most iconic, endearing images that led to an increase in the game's popularity and to the growth of a city. We watched St. Petersburg go from—as one major league baseball owner called it—a "whistle stop little one tank town," to a city that blossomed into a national media center every spring for seven decades.

1

GODFATHER OF FLORIDA BASEBALL

Al Lang was dying. His lungs would not tolerate another Pittsburgh winter. A warm climate, the doctor reasoned, might help extend his time. So, the sanguine Lang sold his very lucrative laundry business, tilted his head toward the sun and headed south.

There are at least four accounts of how the thirty-nine-year-old seemingly half-man, half-myth and his wife, Marie, wound up in St. Petersburg in 1910. Some say by train, others by boat. Some accounts have his first stop in Tampa, others in Fort Myers. The most amusing, in his own words, as told by longtime sportswriter and baseball historian Fred Lieb, goes like this: "I want to buy the Pullman tickets for myself and my wife to somewhere in the South as far as your train runs," Lang told the ticket agent. "In fact, to the very end of the line."

Lang was informed that the end of the line was a little town named St. Petersburg. "If the engineer tried to go any farther, he would plunge into Tampa Bay," the railroad employee told Lang, who to that point had never heard of St. Petersburg. "That sounds like the kind of place I have in mind," he replied.

They arrived at the Atlantic Coast Line station at First Avenue South and Second Street South to find the ticket agent had spoken the truth: the deep blue waters of Tampa Bay lay before them, and right across the street was the property on which he would eventually build two ballparks. Lieb also recounted this conversation between the two Langs. "Feg," Al said to his wife, using his nickname for her, a shortened version of her maiden name, Fagen, "I think I could settle down in this place with you and be happy." "If you would be happy, then I would be happy, too," she answered.

Albert Fielding Lang, or "Sunshine Al," or "Uncle Al," as he came to be known, would live for another fifty years. When he died, the city lost perhaps its most important citizen of the twentieth century and surely its biggest booster. Wrote the *St. Petersburg Evening Independent*, "He was given life by the city's sunshine and repaid the debt by devoting himself to building the city into something better than he found it."

The Sporting News lauded: "Another man might have gone into hibernation and spent most of his waking hours ranting against a cruel destiny which, in the prime of his life, had torn him from his Pittsburgh roots and exiled him among strangers. But Al did not moan. He saw in St. Petersburg an ideal spot for spring training. He was not truly among strangers."

Growing up as one of three kids to John, an alcoholic, and Harriet Lang, Al could often be found three blocks from home at the Monongahela House, where players from the visiting pre-1900s American Association teams stayed when they were playing the hometown Pittsburgh Alleghanys. This infatuation may help explain why Lang possessed less than an eighth-grade education. Rather, he became familiar with the players and became certain

Al Lang and a fan in the early days at Waterfront Park. *Courtesy of St. Petersburg Museum of History.*

of one thing: he wanted to be one, much to the consternation of his family. "Al's idea of a 'good place,'" his brother John told *The Sporting News*, "was where they played big league baseball every day of the year and where one's boon companions were Honus Wagner, Fred Clarke, Tommy Leach and the big league stars of the day."

To cure Al of his acute case of hero worship, the family put him to work at age fourteen, and soon he was driving a wagon for Brace Brothers Laundry. He became consumed by the work, which led him to start his own very successful laundry business, Lincoln Laundry, while in his early twenties. But the work almost killed him. "I was driving myself so hard that I thought I'd never be able to stop," he told Frank Graham of *Sport* magazine in 1951. "The money didn't spur me on. I was only trying to keep up with the new customers we seemed to be gathering by the dozens every day."

In St. Petersburg, he found life wasn't over. On the contrary, for the genial Lang, it was good. "Six months passed and I was more alive than ever," Lang told *The Sporting News*. "A year went by and that doctor in Pittsburgh looked like a sucker. I sat in the sun and reveled in life." After realizing that he had indeed discovered his heaven on earth in St. Petersburg, Lang quickly bought a lot on Beach Drive and Ninth Street North. "I was very happy in my new environment," Lang went on. "But one thing was lacking. I was too far from baseball." He would soon do something about that.

Legendary war correspondent Ernie Pyle, who was writing features for Scripps Howard on a 1935 swing down Florida's west coast, interviewed Lang for two days and wrote the following; "He is, by his own admission, one of the happiest men alive. And why shouldn't he be? He has enough money to do exactly what he wants to do. That consists of two things. Going to baseball games and tooting the horn for St. Petersburg. He is one of the nation's most rabid baseball fans. He is more than just a fan—he is an intimate of everyone in baseball. There isn't a big league player he doesn't know personally. Nor an owner, nor official, nor sports writer. He is part of baseball. And yet, he never played a game in his life outside of sandlots."

Wrote Charles Fountain in *Under the March Sun*, "Lang was the first to realize that spring training would make St. Petersburg a tourist mecca." Lang may not have been the first to see how baseball could help drive tourism, but he was the first to activate it. As far back as November 1908, the *St. Petersburg Times*, which was published on Wednesdays and Saturdays, wrote about the semipro games being played in the Tampa Bay area: "Baseball has this year added not a little to the reputation of St. Petersburg and there is no limiting the distance that any kind of fame travels."

The bespectacled, well-dressed Lang made it his business to know the major league players, owners, executives and media in every city. He hosted baseball parties every spring for them all, the first in 1913. "Few men have ever cherished a town as he cherishes this one," wrote Graham. "No man ever has worked as hard to let the world know of the virtues of his home." When the ubiquitous Lang missed the opening of the 1954 World Series, it was the first time he was absent since its inception in 1903. It was not uncommon for the majority—and in some cases, all—of the datelines on the front page of the springtime editions of the baseball bible, *The Sporting News*, to be from St. Petersburg.

In his first eight years after landing in the city he called "S'Petersurg," he was twice elected mayor with an agenda of improving the city's image aimed squarely at bolstering tourism. In effect, he set the course for the city's future. "Al Lang's tourist-oriented administration represented an important turning point in the city's economic and political history," wrote Raymond Arsenault in his book *St. Petersburg and the Florida Dream*: "From the Lang era onward, the public effort to encourage tourism would be formal and unceasing, in sharp contrast to the sporadic promotional campaigns of earlier years."

Longtime historian and author Gary Mormino wrote in his book *Land of Sunshine, State of Dreams*, "Perhaps no other city in Florida has or had so perfected and refined the importance of image in selling itself." There is little doubt that Lang and John Lodwick played major roles in that evolution. Lodwick was hired by Lang's administration as the city's public relations director, making St. Petersburg the first city anywhere to have such a person, according to Mormino. At the time of Lodwick's death in 1942, Lang declared in the *St. Petersburg Times*, "No man ever did greater work in publicizing the city."

Lang was sworn into office on July 1, 1916, and four days later, he announced a plan to clear all of the incongruous advertising signs hanging over the sidewalks on Central Avenue in order to give the city a more pleasing, consistent pattern. It was Al who initiated the Green Bench Ordinance, requiring all city benches be of a uniform size and repainted, from a variety of colors to dark green. Nevin Sitler, curator, historian and director of education of the St. Petersburg Museum of History, wrote that Lang's benches "paid homage to (the city's) dedication to recuperation, relaxation and recreation." (Once iconic, the benches were removed in 1967 as the city attempted to shake the national media's unfortunate tag of "God's Waiting Room.") As mayor, Lang was also involved in replacing the sand roadways with brick and oversaw the building of the city's open-air post office in 1916.

The major league teams training in St. Petersburg were often involved in the Festival of States parade after Al Lang helped launch it in 1917. *Courtesy of St. Petersburg Museum of History.*

Attempting to compete with other tourist-attracting southern festivals such as Mardi Gras, he and a Phillies scout named William Neale successfully launched the city's first Festival of States in 1917 and then restored it five years later after having been halted by World War I. As mayor, Lang helped establish the St. Petersburg Lawn Bowling Club, the first golf course and helped found the city's first telephone company.

So proud was Lang of the city that, as mayor, he frequently greeted visitors, often in his signature all-white suit, as they stepped from the train. "Lang's years as mayor and the booming twenties that followed were a feel-good, can-do time for St. Petersburg," noted Fountain. Arsenault called Lang "probably the most influential mayor in the city's history."

He was also likely its most generous. Al and Marie had no children of their own, but during one difficult spring season made dark by the Great Depression, a beaming Lang was seen practically skipping down Central Avenue with a young infant, the son of a friend and Al's namesake. The Langs targeted the young with their charity. In 1958, he donated $100,000 in his late wife's name to a children's home in Jacksonville, and in the year before his death he gave $250,000 to Presbyterian College—renamed Eckerd College thirteen years later—with the intent of helping disadvantaged youth receive an education. According to the *St. Petersburg Times*, Lang sent seventeen local students to college and the bulk of his nearly $700,000 estate went to help children medically and educationally. It was reportedly a well-kept secret that Al and Marie would buy a carload of groceries every weekend during the Great Depression and pass them out to needy friends.

His greatest contribution, however, was elsewhere. Lang didn't just bring baseball teams to St. Petersburg; he brought the game's best teams. He didn't just bring the game's best teams; he brought the baseball industry. Most importantly, he didn't just bring the baseball industry; he kept all of it on the waterfront for five decades. And all of them depended on Al—for everything. Finally, he oversaw the building of two ballparks, both considered among the best of their times. It was all necessary, as Lang would say, "in keeping with our importance in the baseball world."

According to a 1928 report in the *St. Petersburg Times*, Yankees owner Colonel Jacob Ruppert confessed that eleven other southern cities had bid to become the team's spring home that year alone. In 1931, Ruppert was pressured to move the team's training site to California for a financial guarantee several times greater than that of St. Pete. A decade later, the team also turned down an offer to train in Hawaii. All were victories for Lang.

As more teams followed Ruppert's lead and came to train in Florida, St. Petersburg became the center of the baseball universe every spring. Lang smiled and welcomed them with open arms. "When a ballclub wanted to find a suitable spot to train in Florida, the president of the club invariably told his business manager, 'Go see Al Lang,'" wrote Lieb. When the Tigers moved to their current spring camp at Lakeland in 1934, the *St. Petersburg Times* wrote: "California has made consistent bids for major league clubs over a period of years and Al Lang has been one of the big reasons why most of these bids have been unsuccessful. During the coming season, 11 major league clubs will train (in Florida) and we are willing to wager that Al Lang has something to do with the decisions of all of the club owners in making this state their winter headquarters."

A headline on March 9, 1949, in *The Sporting News* stated, "Sunshine State Hopes to Lure All 16 Teams by 1950." About that same time, Lang remarked: "It used to be that I had to seek out people and try to sell them on St. Petersburg. The years of hard work are paying off and now people come to me and asked me to talk. I love it." So popular was the idea of training in

Al Lang's green benches on Central Avenue in downtown St. Petersburg. *Courtesy of Library of Congress.*

St. Pete that, according to the *St. Petersburg Times*, Larry MacPhail, president of the Dodgers, spoke to Lang about his team joining the Cardinals and Yankees in St. Petersburg. "Naturally," wrote the *Times*' Stan Witwer, "Lack of [another] ballpark shelved the suggestion, but it just goes to show you how the magnates feel about St. Petersburg as a training site."

Sitler noted that "Lang and Lodwick even encouraged owners and players to sign Major League contracts during spring training making St. Petersburg the dateline for countless sports pages." In 1929, Lang may have outdone himself when he persuaded American League president Ernest Barnard to make St. Petersburg the league's permanent winter headquarters from

November through spring training. After Barnard died suddenly in 1931, Lang was considered a replacement, but Will Harridge was named to the post, a move Lang applauded.

"Before Al Lang came along, St. Petersburg was viewed by baseball as little more than a blip on the map," wrote author and historian Wes Singletary.

Lang wasn't perfect. Lieb described him this way: "He was paradoxical, a contradictory character. He had many virtues, no vices, but many pet hates and peeves. He would sit 45 minutes on a bench awaiting a bus to his last abode on Snell Isle rather than spend the price of a taxi cab, and then go home and write a $25,000 check for his church or some charitable institution." In 1915, during the Phillies' first spring in St. Petersburg at the field at Coffee Pot Bayou, Lang often competed with fans over foul balls, according to historian Robert D. Warrington in his essay "St. Petersburg: Its Beginnings and the Phillies' Experience in 1915." As part of his deal with the team, Lang supplied the baseballs.

Although he glided rather easily along all the avenues of the world of Major League Baseball and was treated like family in the homes of baseball icons such as Connie Mack and Branch Rickey, Lang was not without enemies. More than once, Lang dealt with forces conspiring against him. "Lang fought local prejudices, local political cabals, the animosity of folks who do not like baseball or ball players. But he never quit," wrote *The Sporting News* in 1947. "He never owned a baseball club. He never operated a big league club. He made no rules, guided no magnates or players by regulations. But Lang was a tremendous force in American baseball. Al Lang owned a chunk of our national pastime. And all because he had been militant for the game, militant for Florida and militant for St. Petersburg."

It was indeed Al Lang's town, "fashioned by him almost as surely as if he had built each house, each store, each church with his own hands," wrote Graham. And, except for the four years he served as mayor and perhaps a couple of years as president of the Florida State League, he never once got a dime.

2

A BRIEF BEGINNING

After failing to entice his hometown Pirates to train in St. Petersburg, Al Lang first brought baseball to the city in 1914. But that arrangement with Branch Rickey's St. Louis Browns failed after one year due to a disagreement over finances between the city and the team and a better offer from Houston city officials.

The Philadelphia Phillies, too, were in St. Pete for a short stint before leaving after four years for Charlotte, North Carolina. Opinions differ as to the exact location of the field where these two teams trained, except that it was roughly two miles north of Central Avenue, somewhere in the Coffee Pot Bayou section of St. Petersburg. The effects of World War I had something to do with the Phillies leaving, but it also may have been the lack of other major league clubs to schedule games with. In one of their last games before departing, the Fightin' Phils hosted St. Petersburg High School. The final score was 21–1. Baseball historian Fred Lieb wrote, much to Lang's dismay, that Phillies owner William F. Baker thought St. Petersburg had lost its magic. Finally, it may have been the team's nomadic nature. The Phils trained in eighteen different locations in their first twenty-eight years, and in their first fifty, they remained in only one place as long as their four-year stay in St. Pete: Winter Haven, from 1928 to 1937.

With the Phillies leaving, Mayor Lang went to work right away on a replacement, and on January 24, 1919, it appeared he had found one when the *St. Petersburg Times* declared that the New York Giants were coming to the city for their spring training trip. Giants manager John McGraw had

Giants Hall of Fame
manager John McGraw
(*left*) was on the verge of
bringing his team to train
on the waterfront in 1919
after his counterpart with
the Phillies, Pat Moran (*right*),
had nothing but praise for
the Sunshine City. *Courtesy of
the Library of Congress.*

received positive reports on St. Petersburg, including one from Phillies manager Pat Moran. More hopes were raised when it was learned that the Giants had booked rooms at the Edgewater Inn. The speculation, however, turned out to be just that. Two days later, the team announced that it had instead opted for Gainesville, an arrangement that lasted only one year. Not only was St. Pete still without a team, it also would soon be without a field. The former home of the Browns and Phillies at Coffee Pot Bayou (or Sunshine Park, as it came to be known) would be demolished by the end of March. The five-year-old wood grandstand, without a tenant, was now viewed as a fire hazard by property owner C. Perry Snell. In fact, three fires had been extinguished in the month leading up to the demolition.

Lang had much to do. And while St. Petersburg was largely spared the effects of the Spanish influenza pandemic—unlike Tampa, where three hundred of the city's fifty thousand citizens died—it did require his attention during much of his last two years in office.

In August 1919, he put out a call asking for someone to produce a large tract of land for a ballpark that Lang promised he would turn into a major league spring training site. It wasn't until December that the call was answered. Dr. J.L. Moorefield, who, according to the *St. Petersburg Times*, had arrived in December 1918 from Petersburg, Virginia, and set up his medical practice the following month, had arranged to lease land at Fourth Street and Eighth Avenue South. Moorefield, a baseball enthusiast whose brother George was a catching prospect in the Red Sox organization, secured a guarantee that a field could be built within ten days, which would make it the only regulation field in the city.

Weeks later, the good doctor and Lang nearly coaxed the Yankees to train there, but the team's brass chose to return to Jacksonville for a second year. For the second consecutive January, Lang was spurned by a New York team. Undeterred, Lang and Moorefield lured the American Association's Indianapolis club to train on Moorefield's field. Later, on March 3, 1920, the Florida State League granted St. Pete a franchise.

3

WATERFRONT PARK

The legendary "Shoeless" Joe Jackson, who the exacting Hall of Famer Ted Williams called "as good a player to ever play this game," was coming to St. Petersburg to wear the uniform of the hometown team, the Saints.

Dr. Moorefield, owner of St. Pete's new baseball field, had purchased ownership of the city's entry in the fledgling, fitful Florida West Coast Winter Baseball League. Moorefield had hired Jackson to manage the off-season Saints for the approaching 1920–21 season. The Saints' roots in the city were deep. In October 1908, on a field near what is now Mirror Lake, the semipro Saints played what was likely the first game involving a major league team in St. Petersburg. They fell, 7–0, to the Cincinnati Reds, who were barnstorming their way on a fall trip to Cuba. The Saints were about to get their most famous member.

"Joe Jackson of the Chicago White Sox is going to blossom as a manager this winter," exclaimed *The Sporting News*. "He is to organize and head a team that will play ball at St Petersburg in a Florida Resort League."

Joining Jackson was pitcher Claude "Lefty" Williams, who had won 23 games for the White Sox in 1919 and 22 in 1920 and would no doubt be Jackson's top hurler. The *St. Petersburg Times* gushed over the new league with a three-month schedule, "Our fans should appreciate an opportunity for some winter ball with some big league stars, and we believe they would, and we're reaching out with a glad hand wishing the winter league all the good luck that is due a beginner."

Shoeless Joe Jackson (*left*) and his White Sox teammate Claude "Lefty" Williams were headed for St. Petersburg in 1920 when a Chicago grand jury indicted the two and six teammates for their roles in the Black Sox Scandal of 1919. *Both, courtesy of the Library of Congress.*

But Lady Luck never arrived. On September 28, less than three weeks after Moorefield announced the addition of Jackson and Williams to the press, a Chicago grand jury indicted both players and six of their White Sox teammates in the Black Sox scandal of the 1919 World Series. Moorefield suddenly found himself looking for a new skipper. According to the *Times*, a close friend of Jackson from Greenville, South Carolina, wrote the owner a long letter (Jackson was said to be illiterate) pleading for Shoeless Joe to be kept on, but it didn't help. Jackson and the others were expelled from baseball for life by new commissioner Kenesaw Mountain Landis. And then, somehow, it was about to get even worse for Moorefield. Hamstrung by St. Pete's "blue laws" that at the time prohibited Sunday baseball games, thereby limiting his gate, Moorefield announced in December that he couldn't make payroll and had to give up the club. (Professional baseball games in St. Petersburg were not permitted to be played on Sundays until 1930.) To try to recoup some of the money he had already lost on the winter league, Moorefield hired a crew to dismantle the park in order to sell off the wood from the fences and bleachers.

After Moorefield was forced to walk away from the winter league, the city's leadership under Mayor Noel Mitchell—convinced that baseball was an essential component to the tourist trade—asked for and received funding from local businessmen allowing the Saints to play. With no ballpark, they decided on a location at the bottom of Central Avenue at the waterfront, grounds where the Miller Brothers Circus shows were held each year and where informal games had been played. It was far from being a regulation field, consisting mainly of pebbles and sand. Without the proper time or funding needed for the city to add much-needed clay to the irregular grounds, the media took to calling the home of the winter league Saints the "sandbar," "sand mine" or worse. One advance story in the *St. Petersburg Times* prior to a game between the Saints and the Sarasota squad stated, "the two winter league teams would wrestle with the sandspurs upon the waterfront crater." Regardless, the field's downtown location made it easy for tourists to walk to the games, a key factor in the city officials' decision to move there.

Meanwhile, another plea for baseball funds was about to begin. The St. Petersburg Athletic Association turned its attention to the Florida State League (FSL) version of the Saints and whether they would return for their second season that spring. A fundraising drive led by Al Lang and the president of the association, Robert Carroll, quickly generated support. The goal of $15,000 was reached on March 22, less than a month before the start of the FSL season.

One thing was still needed: a suitable location for a regulation field to replace Moorefield's now-razed park. While the *Times* was leading the fundraising drive, it had long made its position known as to where the park should be located, writing in a 1919 editorial that it was "opposed to putting the Field on the waterfront because it has held and will continue to hold that the waterfront park is St. Petersburg's front yard. It is everybody's lawn. A man does not build his tool shed or his garage in his front yard. The waterfront should be kept clear and free of everything of this character."

However, at an evening meeting on April 1, members of the city's park board voted unanimously to give the athletic association a tract of land lying south of the Atlantic Coast Railroad line, at First Avenue between First Street and the bay, a block or two south of the "crater." Train carloads of clay were immediately on their way to the site to prepare the grounds for the team's FSL opener, scheduled for April 25. Three days later, lumber arrived for the grandstand. The following day, the venue's foundation was laid. Job foreman Bob Sharp put out a call for carpenters, who were to be paid in tickets to FSL games that summer. As time began to grow short, another call for carpenters was issued. The clay arrived on April 15, and work began on the infield. Just two days before the opener, the *St. Petersburg Times* erected a scoreboard on the site that included tracking all out-of-town FSL games. In twenty-four days' time, Waterfront Park was born and ready for the Saints' home opener against the Tampa Smokers.

In the first game, the Saints defeated the Smokers, 10–1, scoring six runs in the first inning before a crowd so large it overflowed onto the field, making ground rules necessary. Any ball hit into the right-field crowd was considered a double. The first batter was the Smokers' forty-four-year-old player-manager, Tommy Leach, a veteran of nineteen major league seasons as an outfielder and a likely Gold Glove winner had those coveted trophies been awarded at the time. Tampa hit the park's first home run, described this way by the *St. Petersburg Times*: "with two out in the eighth inning, Eachman lost one of Wilson's hops in the sand down around the oleander bushes in deep left field."

The final piece of the puzzle was put in place on July 16, when the baseball association, the city and the Atlantic Coast Line Railroad (which owned a portion of the property on which the ballpark sat) agreed to a ninety-nine-year lease on the new field, which would also be used by the city's grammar and high school teams.

4

BRAVES BECOME THE FIRST AND ADD TO ST. PETE'S BOOM

O n March 13, 1920, Al Lang announced that he would not seek a
third term as mayor of St. Petersburg. It was the same day that the
American Association's Indianapolis Indians made their spring debut
in the city at the new Moorefield Park by hosting Southern College. If
nothing else, it served as an unwelcome reminder to Lang that there would
be no major league team calling St. Pete home for the second consecutive
spring. The Washington Senators, in Tampa, were the only team training
in the Tampa Bay area.

It was one of the few unhappy periods in Lang's life, according to Fred
Lieb. "We aren't any town for minor league teams to train in," he quoted
Lang as saying.

City officials didn't disagree. In a 1993 article entitled "Spring Training
and Publicity in the Sunshine City," Melissa Keller wrote:

*For St. Petersburg, the experience with spring training in 1914–1918
offered new opportunities for advertising and tourism. City promoters
considered baseball a powerful source of publicity. Although local
leaders praised spring training's ability to attract visitors, actual figures
on tourism generated from spring baseball are nonexistent. Tangible
numbers, even if available, would not likely change the evidence. St.
Petersburg city leaders, including editors and elected officials, clearly
believed spring training could attract more favorable publicity than
nearly any other inducement St. Petersburg had to offer, except perhaps,*

sunshine. In addition to forming a part of the city's economic structure, spring training also contributed to the city's sense of identity. One editor made this clear during the 1920s when he stated, "So well known is St. Petersburg that in Boston and New York newspapers the name of the state is not carried in their telegraphic datelines. There is only one St. Petersburg to the baseball fans." For St. Petersburg, this statement epitomized everything local leaders and private citizens wanted from spring training—national recognition and publicity.

Per usual, Lang was at the 1920 and 1921 World Series, moving freely among the league owners and executives and chatting up his beloved city. He was determined to end the drought of major league baseball on the waterfront. According to Fred Lieb, "He (Lang) heard that the Boston Braves were dissatisfied with their camp in Galveston, Texas and pitched owner George Washington Grant on the advantages of St. Petersburg's training weather." Working on behalf of the city, Lang no doubt enlisted the help of some of his many friends in baseball to apply pressure on the Braves.

The November 6, 1921 edition of the *St. Petersburg Times* noted that there were two major league teams interested in coming to the Sunshine City the following spring: the Cincinnati Reds and the Boston Braves. Lang favored the Braves, an advertising market trailing only New York and Chicago.

But as the darkness of winter descended on the Sunshine City, Lang had nothing official, no major league team lined up for 1922. It was eleven days before Christmas when the city's tireless ambassador received the joyful news from the Braves via telegram that they had agreed to train in St. Pete. Lang's efforts nosed out rivals in Macon, Georgia; Charleston, South Carolina; Orlando, Florida; and, according to sources, "a number of Texas towns." Some of the cities offered a financial incentive to the Braves—common practice at that time. Lang offered no such a thing; only the promise of comfortable weather and first-class facilities.

The deal hinged on whether the city could make the necessary major league upgrades to Waterfront Park's field, grandstand and clubhouse in time for the Braves' March 5 arrival. Satisfactory hotel accommodations were also needed. Lang virtually guaranteed it all on January 9, when the St. Petersburg Chamber of Commerce's Board of Governors agreed to loan $2,500 to the St. Pete Athletic Association to complete improvements to the park. The Braves became the fourth team to conduct spring training

Waterfront Park as it looked in 1922, its first season with Major League Baseball. *Courtesy of St. Petersburg Museum of History.*

in Florida in 1922, joining the Senators (Tampa), Phillies (Leesburg) and Dodgers (Jacksonville). As the *St. Petersburg Times* noted gleefully "They've cut the tax rate by six percent in Pittsburgh, but even that wouldn't take Al Lang back to the smoke and grime."

By the time the Braves arrived, the finished wooden ballpark was hailed as "the finest athletic field in the state if not the entire south," according to Fountain in *Under the March Sun.* The grandstand, which had blown over during the devastating hurricane of October 1921, was rebuilt on a larger scale to seat 1,200, with twenty private boxes, wide and convenient entrances and exits, two box offices, parking for twenty-five cars and toilets for both sexes. The clubhouse, too, was state of the art, with lockers and shower and lavatory facilities. The Braves' hotel accommodations were also first-class. The Edgewater Inn at Seventh Street and Beach Drive featured an elevator and steam heating for the cooler March nights and was an easy walk to the ballpark.

And Lang, according to the *St. Petersburg Times,* was planning "many good times for the major leaguers during their training campaign obtaining courtesies for the athletes from the elegant St. Petersburg Yacht Club and the Coffee Pot Bayou Golf club." Mayor Frank Pulver also had some pleasant surprises in store for the Braves.

The new arrivals stepped off the Atlantic Coast Line in downtown St. Petersburg in the late afternoon of March 5 and were greeted by a crowd of 3,000, including Lang and the mayor. The Braves spent the rest of their evening sightseeing on Central Avenue. The following day, the major leaguers officially stepped on the field at Waterfront Park for their first workout. The weather was so nice for their 10:00 a.m. session that Manager Fred Mitchell unexpectedly scheduled another for later in the afternoon. The home opener against the Tampa-based Washington Senators was scheduled for March 21, but two days before, the two teams met at Tampa's Plant Field. The Braves won before 2,188 fans. According to the *Times*, a Tampa fan insisted that the Boston Beaneaters wouldn't draw a "corporal's guard" for the rematch in St. Pete. The longtime rivalry between the two cities was on. The headline on the front page of the *Times* the day of the game threw out a challenge: "Wanted: 5,000 Baseball Fans to Make Tampa Look Sickish."

In the first major league game at Waterfront Park, Washington trounced the Braves, 7–3. The Nats roughed up Braves starter Rube Marquard (HOF 1971), who was making his Braves debut after winning 17 games the year before for Cincinnati. Washington's starter, George Mogridge, allowed just 1 run in four innings. A capacity crowd of 2,223 witnessed the game, eclipsing Tampa's Opening Day gate by 35.

Meanwhile, for the second consecutive spring, the future of the 1922 FSL Saints was uncertain, due to financial shortfalls. On April 1, St. Petersburg Athletic Club president Robert Carroll announced the need for help. Attendance at the early games, he warned, would be crucial. Not only did St. Pete's baseball boosters respond well, so did the Saints, who went on to win the city's first championship on the upgraded diamond on the waterfront.

While the city was already primed for a big tourist season, the Braves' presence undoubtedly had an impact. The 1921–22 tourist season attracted the highest number of visitor registrations in St. Petersburg's history. It was clear that the city was entering a period of fantastic growth. According to figures released by the U.S. Census Bureau, St. Petersburg's population increased 277.5 percent (14,237 to 39,504) from 1920 to 1930. In his book *Mangroves to Major League*, Rick Baker stated that "real estate valuation for the city increased 300% from 1920 through 1925." By 1924, the number of major league teams training in Florida had grown to nine, more than double the number just three years before. The headline in the *Times* on March 23, 1924, could have been penned by Lang himself: "St. Petersburg Gets Wide Publicity for Baseball."

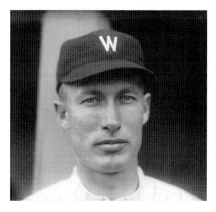 

Left: After first participating in the Festival of States parade on March 30, 1922, Washington's Hall of Fame right fielder Sam Rice hit the first and only home run of the first season on the waterfront, a 3-run shot to give the Senators a 5–2 win. *Courtesy of the Library of Congress.*

Right: Hall of Famer Rube Marquard pitched four scoreless innings to save the lowly Braves' improbable 1–0 win over the defending 1923 National League champion New York Giants, with seven future Hall of Famers of their own. *Courtesy of the Library of Congress.*

• • • •

March 30, 1922

Players from the Senators and Braves participated in the Festival of States parade as their motorcade traveled down Central Avenue to the park for their 3:00 p.m. game. Later, future Hall of Famer Sam Rice (HOF 1963) hit the first and only home run of the first season on the waterfront, a three-run shot to give the Senators a 5–2 win.

March 27 and April 3, 1923

Two of the most feared hitters in baseball—the Cardinals' Rogers Hornsby (HOF 1942) and the Indians' player-manager, Tris Speaker (HOF 1937)—made their Waterfront Park debuts in the same week. Hornsby, seven-time and reigning National League batting champion, drilled 2 key singles in the Cards' 3–0 win over the host Braves, who were held to 1 hit by three Redbird hurlers. One week later, Speaker, who batted .300 or better eighteen times in his career and who carried a .346 career batting average into the 1923 spring training season, made an immediate impact. On the third pitch of his first at bat, Speaker hit a screaming line drive to right field that got past another Hall of Famer, the Braves' Billy Southworth (HOF 2008), and rolled under the fence for a pre–ground rules homer in the Indians' 12–11 win.

March 22, 1924
In one of the greatest pitching performances ever at Waterfront Park, the 100-loss Boston Braves defeated the defending National League champion New York Giants, 1–0. Joe Genewich and Rube Marquard (HOF 1971) scattered 7 hits while shutting out a lineup that featured seven future Hall of Fame position players. Approximately 4,500 fans were jammed in and around the park while waiting two hours for the visiting Giants to arrive from Sarasota. The team attempted to take the Bee Line Ferry from Manatee, but rough Tampa Bay waters forced them to return. The group instead arrived in a parade of cars. Billy Southworth tripled on the first pitch of the game for the Giants but was stranded. The Braves scored the only run of the game in the sixth on an RBI double to right by left fielder Bill Cunningham. Marquard earned the win with four scoreless innings.

April 5, 1924
In his only career appearance at Waterfront Park, Walter Johnson, with 354 career wins at the time, threw five innings and allowing 1 run but did not get the decision in the Senators' 4–3 win over the Braves. In his eighteenth season, the thirty-six-year-old Johnson would go on to win American League MVP honors and lead the AL in wins (23), ERA (2.72) and strikeouts (159), and the Nats would go on to win Johnson's only World Series title.

5

THE "DISCOVERY" OF ST. PETERSBURG

I t was the beginning of storm season in St. Petersburg, and on this Monday night in June 1924, the season delivered. Despite the rain, more than one hundred people ventured outside to attend a meeting of the city commission at City Hall. Inside was a discussion that would be the most important to the city's baseball fortunes for the next seventy years. Three days before, Al Lang, head of the city's baseball committee, had secured an agreement to bring the defending world champion Yankees to St. Pete for the 1925 spring training season. To entice the world's most recognizable sports franchise with an equally recognizable right fielder was perhaps the coup of a lifetime. It wasn't easy. Yankees owner Colonel Jacob Ruppert was skeptical at first.

According to baseball writer and historian Fred Lieb, Ruppert asked, "Why should a sensible man want to leave a 400,000 town like New Orleans where we get good money for our exhibitions, for your little one-horse town?" But Lang pushed on.

Two things helped: the advocacy of Yankees manager Miller Huggins, who shared a house with his sister Myrtle on Twelfth Avenue North; and the Yankees' desire to get the philandering, self-indulgent Babe Ruth out of New Orleans, their training site for the previous four years. Lang had sold Huggins on the virtues of St. Petersburg, even convincing the former law student to purchase multiple properties there for himself. Huggins's first trip to the city may have been in 1908 as the diminutive starting second baseman for the barnstorming Cincinnati Reds team that played the city's semipro team, the Saints.

Yankees manager Miller Huggins was helpful to Al Lang in getting the Yankees to move their training camp from New Orleans to St. Petersburg in 1925. *Courtesy of the Library of Congress.*

The Yankees' contract, however, was contingent on the city building a training field for the team at Crescent Lake Park, and that was the matter at hand at City Hall that inclement evening. As early as 1916, Lang began setting his sights on bringing a New York team to the city, but both the Giants and Yankees had already turned him down. Having the Braves in St. Pete didn't dimmish that yearning. According to the *St. Petersburg Times*, he told the city's chamber of commerce: "No town in the country except Hot Springs has ever had two ball clubs training within its limits at one time. We have the Braves. Let's go after the Yankees."

With the damp throng looking on inside the meeting room at Central Avenue and Fourth Street, the city's six-member commission voted unanimously to fund the Yankees' training headquarters for $40,000. And just like that, the little bayside village that Lang settled in thirteen years before was about to become baseball's most important city every spring for decades to come.

Four words streaked across the top of the *St. Petersburg Times* the next morning: "Yankees Coming to City." According to the *Times*, a professional publicist at the meeting estimated the publicity value of the announcement to be $250,000 (roughly $4,000,000 today). It was also believed that a single story in a New York paper was worth approximately $13,000 ($200,000 today).

Twelve days later, at a meeting at the Yankees' offices, Lang, referred to as the "Godfather of Florida Baseball" by the *New York Telegram Mail*, Huggins and the team's business manager, Ed Barrow, agreed to a six-year contract. "The Yankees," according to the *Telegram Mail*, had "become real tired of New Orleans after four years, and longed for something different." Al Lang promised them they would get it in St. Petersburg.

The excitable Lang immediately began making plans to send the city's own Pullman train car to Boston and New York to fetch the media members who covered the teams. Reasoned the *St. Petersburg Evening Independent*, "While it would be impossible to bring the members of the two teams south in the special Pullman, the fact that the newspapermen traveled in

'Sunshine' would be worth almost as much in securing newspaper space in the metropolitan papers."

Over the years, those same New York newspapermen took to ribbing Lang by referring to the start of Yankees spring training each year as "the anniversary of the discovery of St. Petersburg."

Conversely, Babe Ruth's reaction mirrored that of other Yankees players, who loved the fact that the Big Easy tended to look the other way when it came to the Volstead Act. "Why in the heck does anybody want to train in a town like that?" asked Ruth. "That's an old man's town, ain't it?"

Ironically, no one would come to enjoy St. Petersburg like Ruth, who spent much of his free time there golfing, fishing and hunting. In five of his last six seasons with the Yankees, Ruth celebrated his February 6 birthday not in New York, but with lavish parties at the local Jungle Country Club Hotel.

Including newspapermen, front office staff and uniformed personnel, the Yankees' spring training party would number almost one hundred. The first group pulled into the Seaboard Air Line train station at Ninth Street and First Avenue South in St. Petersburg on Sunday, February 22, 1925. A light rain fell as they were met by Lang in white flannels and straw hat and a large crowd on that Sunday morning. Taxis took them the eight blocks to the Princess Martha Hotel, where they were welcomed by a Scottish Highlander band dressed in kilts and bearskins. The next day, Lang, on behalf of the city, officially presented the Yankees with their new practice facility at Crescent Lake. According to the *St. Petersburg Times*, nearly five thousand fans showed up, prompting the city to quickly install additional bleachers in time for the team's first workout the following day. Babe Ruth had not yet arrived from his annual retreat to Hot Springs and wasn't present at the ceremony, but his wife, Helen, and daughter, Dorothy were there representing him before leaving early.

Featuring a 390-foot fence in right field, the park was made with Babe Ruth in mind. With a short porch or even normal dimensions to Ruth's power field, the game's all-time home run hitter, the Yankees reasoned, could easily hit twenty-five balls over the fence and into the park's alligator-infested lake during the daily workouts. At two dollars a ball, even the mighty Yankees kept count of their practice balls. Still, in his book *The Making of St. Petersburg*, Will Michaels wrote that, in 1926, the Crescent Lake ballpark outfield was extended to keep Ruth's mammoth blasts inside the park. It didn't work. "On a single day in 1928," wrote Michaels, "Babe hit six balls into the lake. Crescent Lake was then 530 feet from home plate at the right field line."

Babe Ruth found outdoor life to his liking in St. Petersburg. *Courtesy of the Library of Congress.*

Historian Tim Reid likened Ruth's arrival in the city on March 1 to that of the Beatles at Kennedy Airport forty years later. In his book, Michaels called it "Ruthmania" and included this description of Ruth's arrival from the *New York Times*: "The earthquake in Northern regions yesterday was a mild little affair compared to the reverberating tremors which shook St. Petersburg when the Sultan of Swat joined the social colony here. The occasion marked the official start of the baseball and social season on the west coast. All the beauty and chivalry of St. Petersburg on hand to welcome the great Babe and his progress from the [Seaboard station]to the Princess Martha was nothing less than a triumphal march."

The Bambino stepped off the train to a raucous welcome, featuring a lively band rendition of "Hail to the Chief." Ruth arrived with a bulldog in his arms, a gift for his beloved daughter, Dorothy, who met him at the train.

According to the *St. Petersburg Times*, the New York media was not kind to the Sunshine City in their early dispatches from the Yankees' camp. In reflecting on their arrival that first year, Hy Goldberg of the *Newark Evening News* later wrote that moving their training camp from New Orleans to St. Petersburg was "like leaping from a carousel into a monastery, from a city infused with the Mardi Gras spirit into a quiet peace-loving community. Sportswriters twitted [not tweeted] the place in their daily dispatches. They wrote 'funny' pieces about a 'city on wheelchairs.' But they subsequently discovered that the older generation, having seen and heard much, doesn't make a bad selection when it seeks a place to live."

Four days after the Yankees arrived, twenty Braves reached St. Petersburg on the last Thursday evening of February and were met by Al Lang but few others. Soon after, due to a previous engagement and the uncooperating weather, Lang was unable to attend the Braves' first workout. It didn't go unnoticed by the press, among others.

Given that Lang was also serving as the president of the wobbly Florida State League and was pitching in vain the idea of another Florida winter league to the presidents of the American and National Leagues, his absence may have been forgiven.

But Lang and the city's chamber of commerce staff reacted quickly to the sleight, suggesting a citywide parade for the New Englanders. However, Braves manager Dave Bancroft dismissed the idea. "We're here to play ball," he was quoted in the *St. Petersburg Times*. He did agree to a celebration, provided it was held at the ballpark. Braves Day at Waterfront Park occurred on March 9 amid rumors that the team was considering Miami as a future spring home.

From left to right: Lou Gehrig; Dick Mayes, a fan from Brooksville, Florida; and Babe Ruth prior to a game at Waterfront Park. *Courtesy of St. Petersburg Museum of History*.

On a warm breezy Monday afternoon, approximately 4,500 Braves backers showed up for the ballyhooed free event that amounted to a few speeches and a six-inning intrasquad game. At game's end, Lang announced that an agreement had been reached: The Braves would remain on the waterfront for the next five years. Bancroft would later say, "I have trained in California, Texas, Alabama, in fact in nearly all the states in which ball clubs hold spring training. But there isn't a place in the United States that can equal Petersburg, not only for climate and training facilities, but also for the treatment the club receives." By spring's end, Ruppert had announced that the Yankees, too, would gladly be returning. "I like St. Petersburg better than any city in which we have ever taken the Yankees," he was quoted as saying in the *St. Petersburg Times*. "Never before have I stayed more than two days in a training camp. I have been here two weeks."

Peace had been kept in the Sunshine City, even if it lasted only as long as October. After such an agreeable spring, who knew the Yankees would go on to post a 69-85 regular-season record in 1925, their worst in twelve years? According to *The Sporting News*, the mercurial Ruppert scolded Huggins after the season: "Why did you let that fellow Al Lang sell me on St. Petersburg? We train three years in New Orleans and win pennants and we go to St.

Petersburg and almost finish last." As it turned out, the Yankees won the next three American League pennants and two World Series. That 1925 team was the only Yankee squad to finish in the second division during their four decades in St. Pete. As for Ruppert, he would spend many a fine spring vacations in Al Lang's paradise.

When the St. Petersburg boom turned into an economic slump in 1926, the presence of two teams from two of the country's top three media markets was never more important, as the city began to rely even more heavily on tourists from the North to supply the local economy. Babe Ruth's presence didn't hurt, either. Everyone seemed to benefit. On March 18, 1925, the St. Petersburg Kennel Club held the Babe Ruth Cup Race, and five thousand fans attended, the track's largest crowd ever. In his book *Babe Ruth in Florida*, Kevin McCarthy wrote: "To say that George Herman was the whole show would not be a distortion of the truth. When he was out of the lineup in an exhibition game, either because of injury or a previous engagement, promoters had to apologize and assure the fans that the Bambino would be playing the next game."

After the Yankees' first spring at Waterfront Park, the city's Rotarians voted to contribute $4,100 to the team to make up the difference between the total gate receipts and the guarantee. Al Lang's personal $250 donation was the largest individual offering. He blamed the shortfall on Ruth missing a game and two other games played in poor weather. No one complained. The Yankees' eight games on the Waterfront represented the greatest publicity campaign in the city's history, and its financial windfall was incalculable.

In the spring following the 1927 legendary Murderer's Row 110-win season, St. Petersburg set its tourism record, including a record number of visitors from New York. Later that year, the St. Petersburg City Council authorized the construction of Albert Whitted Airport, adjacent to Waterfront Park. It opened the following summer, further catering to the tourists.

• • • •

March 12, 1925
In their first game at Waterfront Park, the Yankees beat the Braves, 14–10, after trailing 6–0 and 10–6. A crowd of five thousand squeezed onto the grounds. Babe Ruth was not in the lineup, the result of an injured finger, but it would be the only home game he would miss that spring. He did judge a series of boxing matches the night before the game. Right fielder Earle Combs (HOF 1970)

had 4 of the Yankees' 20 hits. The game featured 7 doubles and 5 triples, including a bases-loaded three-bagger by New York's Wally Pipp.

March 24, 1925
Babe Ruth hit his first career home run at Waterfront Park, 1 of only 13 he hit in eleven seasons of calling the big park home. This one came in a losing effort to the Dodgers, who pummeled the Yanks, 10–5. Reigning National League home run champ Jack Fornier hit a home run and 2 singles to lead the Brooklyn offense.

March 19, 1926
The Braves and Yankees played to a 6–6 tie in twelve innings in a game that was called on account of darkness. The afternoon featured Babe Ruth crashing 2 long doubles and Lou Gehrig's ejection from the game along with six other Yankees by rabbit-eared umpire Frank Wilson for arguing balls and strikes. And, oh yes, an airplane crashed into Tampa Bay beyond the bleachers on the third-base side. One hundred or so fans left their seats to head for the scene, but the two occupants could be seen emerging from the cockpit as the plane sank slowly into the water.

March 17, 1927
In his only game in St. Petersburg, Ty Cobb (HOF 1936), in his first season with Connie Mack's Philadelphia A's after twenty-two years with Detroit, was ejected in the fourth inning of the game against the Boston Braves by home plate umpire Frank Wilson for arguing balls and strikes from the bench. Such a ruckus ensued that the game was eventually forfeited and a seven-inning "practice game" was played immediately after—without the

fiery Cobb, who was later fined $100 by Commissioner Kenesaw Mountain Landis.

Ty Cobb was a member of Connie Mack's Philadelphia A's when he was ejected from his only game in St. Petersburg in 1927. *National Baseball Hall of Fame and Museum photo.*

March 23, 1927
Babe Ruth hit 2 home runs, a double, reached base five times and scored 4 runs, and Lou Gehrig added a triple, 2 singles and scored 3 as the Yankees beat the Braves, 16–7. Ruth hit a home run over the fence and another under. The next day, Gehrig slugged 2 doubles and a triple in a 10–9 loss to the Braves.

March 28, 1927
In Waterfront Park's first battle of defending league champions, the world champion Cardinals knocked off the American League champion Yankees, 5–4. The game was held on the same day as the city's Seventh Annual Festival of States. It would be the first of 138 meetings in St. Petersburg between the two. Cardinals ace Grover Cleveland Alexander, in his seventeenth season and already the owner of more than 300 career wins, pitched seven innings against the starting cast of the powerful '27 Yankees and allowed only 2 hits and no runs and faced just nineteen batters over his last six innings. Twenty-five years later, Ronald Reagan played Alexander in the movie of his storied life, *The Winning Team.*

March 27, 1928
Baseball's first major Cuban star, Reds right-hander Dolph Luque, shut out the Yankees over the last four innings and earned a 6–4 win.

March 2, 1930
The Yankees and Braves announced that, for the first time, fans could purchase season tickets for all games played at Waterfront for the 1930 season.

March 8, 1930
Yankees third baseman Ben Chapman hit what may have been baseball's first "splash" home run, and Lou Gehrig added a home run and a single as the Bronx Bombers defeated the Braves, 12–9, in the spring opener before six thousand fans. Chapman had 4 hits, including his blast in the second inning that bounced into Tampa Bay, seventy years before they became the rage at San Francisco's AT&T Park.

March 16, 1930

For the first time in the city's history, a professional baseball game was played on Sunday. The Braves defeated the Yankees, 4–1. The Bombers managed 5 hits, including a triple and a single by Lou Gehrig and a single by Babe Ruth. Florida enacted the law to allow those who worked during the week to see Sunday games, no doubt increasing the popularity of the sport among the working class.

March 10, 1931

With two outs and the bases loaded and the score tied in the bottom of the eighth inning, Lou Gehrig dropped a bunt down the third-base line, and the winning run scored in the Yankees' 6–5 win over the Braves. Babe Ruth made a game-saving catch in right field in the ninth.

March 11, 1931

The Yankees trailed the Braves, 8–2, entering the seventh inning but won, 17–9, after scoring 9 unearned runs in the ninth. In the seventh, Gehrig was hit in the head by a throw from second baseman Freddie Maguire as he went into second base and was knocked unconscious. Unfazed, the Iron Horse stayed in the game and delivered a 2-run double in the ninth.

March 24, 1931

Founded in 1930, St. Petersburg's own Kids and Kubs played their first game at Waterfront Park as part of the annual Festival of States. No score was reported.

6

AL LANG VS.
THE GREAT DEPRESSION

On March 4, 1933, just as the Braves and Yankees were reporting to camp and the Great Depression was tightening its grip on the country, newly elected president Franklin D. Roosevelt issued an executive order closing all banks and ordering citizens to turn in to the Treasury Department all of their gold coins, notes and certificates. Acting quickly to relieve the financial situation caused by the nationwide bank holiday, St. Petersburg merchants agreed to accept scrip from those who put up secured collateral, making the city likely the first in the state to do so. Circulation of $75,000 in scrip denominations of $1, $5 and $10 was set up through a clearinghouse established at the American Bank and Trust Company building on Central Avenue, between Third and Fourth Streets, just a few blocks from Waterfront Park.

Many of those in line for the new form of currency were tourists, and of that group, a good number were Braves fans from New England. Bill Cunningham from the *Boston Post* described his journey south, "through snow, ice and financial misery," to reach St. Petersburg, where he was "enwrapped all at once in the sweet and plentitude of warmth that they have here in the land of the pelican. You see those green numbered [Massachusetts] license plates on every third or fourth car," he continued, "and it gives you sort of a 'Howdy brother,' wallop every time you pass one."

Those serving in the business of baseball may also have been standing in those scrip lines, for they were no less immune. Even the players, who received their paychecks only during the regular season, felt the strain.

"Financial distress," wrote the *New York Times*, "was acute among both players and writers because of the situation. It is impossible at the moment to cash any checks and the new theme song with the Dodgers is 'Brother can you spare a dime?'"

In March 1951, Hall of Fame sportswriter Frank Graham from *Sport Magazine* recalled the spring of 1933: "an operation such as the maintenance of a major league training camp, is financed almost solely by checks. All of a sudden, there came the day when a check written by [Yankees owner Colonel Jacob] Ruppert, even for a dollar, was worthless. Bills had to be paid by the club, in cash. Some of the players and three or four of the newspapermen had their families with them and were living in homes leased for the season. Few of them has much cash in hand and their checks, of course were as worthless as Ruppert's."

The St. Petersburg baseball community turned to one man.

Graham continued:

> One group of Yankees and the newspapermen accompanying them, of whom I was one, never will forget the speed with which Al Lang rushed to their rescue. With the consent of the city fathers, he drew thousands of dollars in hard and paper money out of the treasury leaving his personal note as a pledge that it would be repaid. Scorning IOUs, he loaned the money to Ruppert and to the players and reporters. Moreover, he got a list of the stores at which the players' wives traded and set up credit for them, assuming sole responsibility for their debts.

Years later, Lang, of course, shrugged it off, telling Graham: "It was the least I could do for my friends. Every penny of the money was repaid and no merchant who sold his goods on credit lost a penny either."

One of the cost-cutting measures enacted by Major League Baseball was decreasing the number of spring training games while focusing more on training days. There were 267 games scheduled in 1933, 98 fewer than the previous spring. The schedule of games at Waterfront was reduced only slightly, from 19 to 17. A testimonial dinner and public reception honoring both the Yankees and the Braves was canceled due to financial concerns.

The unemployment situation in St. Petersburg was bad, but "not nearly as acute as that of hundreds of industrial cities throughout the nation," wrote Tampa Bay historian Karl Grismer.

Still, in his book *Babe Ruth in Florida*, Kevin McCarthy noted, "Hundreds of young men tried out for teams in spring training not with any real hope of making the teams, but simply for any kind of a job or at least for some good meals before they resumed their place among the unemployed."

On March 14, the Yankees and Braves kicked off the spring schedule at Waterfront Park. The defending world champs managed just 4 hits and lost to the Braves, 4–2, without Ruth, still on a contract holdout. The crowd was estimated at only two thousand. Two days before, Ruth and his partner won a charity golf tournament benefiting the American Legion Crippled Children's Hospital. Some of the young patients were able to meet the Babe on the course.

After the opener, Lang struck again, announcing lower ticket prices for the remaining games at Waterfront Park. "It was decided," wrote the *St. Petersburg Times*, "that because of the (financial) emergency that a scale of prices within the reach of all should prevail and the New York and Boston clubs were pleased to cooperate with Mr. Lang." The Yankees even announced plans to add ten thousand more fifty-cent seats to their own Yankee Stadium.

Meanwhile, Babe Ruth remained unsigned. Wrote the *Times*, "If Ruth persists, observers have pointed out that he would be the only man in the country unwilling under present conditions either to work 'or play' for $50,000." While Ruth had not said what it would take to get him signed, he turned down that amount from Ruppert. The combination of the economics of the times and Ruth's absence kept the crowds thin.

While Ruth may have been absent, the brand of baseball being played on the waterfront was nonetheless spectacular. In a five-day span, two Cardinals bound for Cooperstown—Dizzy Dean and Ducky Medwick—starred in a pair of wins at Waterfront Park. On Saturday, March 18, Dean pitched five hitless innings for the victory, and Medwick—still the last National League player to win the Triple Crown—tripled in his first at bat at Waterfront Park, and the Gashouse Gang beat the Braves, 2–0. Four days later, Medwick's home run off Lefty Gomez gave the Cardinals and Dean a 3–2 win over the defending World Series champion Yankees. And there was even much-needed comedy when actor and filmmaker Buster Keaton hammed it up while going 0-for-1 with 2 walks as a third baseman for the Coca-Cola team in the St. Petersburg Diamond League—the early version of softball—before three thousand admirers in a night game at South Waterfront Park.

Finally, on March 24, after missing nine games, including six home games, Ruth ended his longest holdout, signing his contract in the morning for $52,000, a $23,000 pay cut. That afternoon on the waterfront, the Bambino homered to right field off the Braves' Bob Brown in his second at bat as the Yankees won, 7–1. The crowd was estimated at three times more than any previous game in 1933.

One of those writers feeling the pinch was the *New York Herald Tribune*'s Rud Rennie, who was down to his last $8.75 before help arrived. Rennie was covering the Yankees in 1933 and 1934 and saw a shocking difference between the two spring trainings. "We came home that year [1933] through Southern cities that looked as though they had been ravaged by an invisible enemy," wrote Rennie in the June 16, 1934 *Literary Digest*. "People seemed to be hiding. They would not even come out for Babe Ruth and Lou Gehrig. They simply did not have the money to waste on baseball or amusements."

What a difference a year made. "If the ballclub had not arranged transportation for me in advance [in 1934]," continued Rennie, "I would have had difficulty buying space on a train. People were going to Florida in carloads." Validating Rennie's claim was St. Petersburg's announcement in April that it had again broken the city's tourism mark, beginning a run of six straight years of increased tourist registrations.

Wrote the St. Petersburg Museum of History's Nevin Sitler: "St. Petersburg's Chamber of Commerce, and its army of specialists employed to exploit the sunshine claimed over 150,000 guests for the 1934–35 tourist season. St. Petersburg's sunshine fever was nearly as contagious as the national pastime of baseball. And St. Petersburg had both."

For eighteen months beginning in 1934, the sun never failed to shine over St. Pete. PR whiz John Lodwick and the city's chamber of commerce pumped out bulletins that labeled St. Petersburg as the perfect place to wait out the Depression. "Reports soon circulated," wrote Sitler, "claiming the post-holiday influx of winter visitors in 1933–1934 was the largest in the history of the sport."

Speaking at a St. Petersburg Rotary Club luncheon on March 17, 1933, New York sportswriter Buck O'Neill said: "If you don't believe the city profits from having the New York Yankees here each season, look on the streets at the number of automobiles with New York license plates. It is no accident they are here—it is the result of a carefully conceived and brilliantly executed plan to bring a group here that will spread the fame and benefits of the city."

Historian and author Raymond Arsenault told me, "Although I never searched for any hard evidence to back up my claim, I have often argued that St. Pete came out of the Great Depression relatively early, largely because spring training buoyed the tourist trade in the winter and early spring. My conclusion is based, in part, on the extraordinary popularity of the major league teams in the 1930s. If the teams training in St. Pete had been less popular, I believe the economic and cultural effect would have been much less powerful."

• • • •

March 20, 1934
Fifty Boy Scouts representing eighteen states and the District of Columbia were guests of Babe Ruth for three days in the Sunshine City, but they arrived late to the game and missed the Bambino stroke a long, 2-run triple to right that keyed a 4-run first for the Yankees in their 6–5 win over the Braves. Ruth sent each boy home with crates of oranges and grapefruits.

March 25, 1934
Babe Ruth homered off the Braves' Huck Betts, and legend has it that it may have been his longest. It is believed that Ruth's blast struck the second-floor porch of the Braves' hotel headquarters, the West Coast Inn. It was the last of 13 home runs Ruth hit during his career at cavernous Waterfront Park. The West Coast Inn, which was demolished in 1967, was on the approximate site now occupied by the St. Pete Hilton, across First Street South, some six hundred feet from home plate, which at Waterfront Park was located in what is now the parking lot of Al Lang. According to a *Boston Herald* report, Ruth sent a pitch from Betts "10,000 leagues to right field," carrying "far over the canvas and almost into the West Coast Inn."

March 28, 1934
Future Hall of Fame shortstop Walter "Rabbit" Maranville, one of baseball's more animated figures, suffered multiple fractures of his left leg while colliding with Yankees catcher Norman Kies. The 155-pound, forty-two-year-old Maranville sustained the injury while scoring the tying run on the front end of a double steal in the eighth inning. According to the *St. Petersburg Times*, several fans fainted at the sight of the injury. Braves owner Judge Emil Fuchs deemed it "inadvisable the continuance of the contest," which ended in a 3–3 tie. While white-coated ambulance personnel

Future Hall of Fame shortstop Walter "Rabbit" Maranville suffered what was essentially a career-ending injury and likely the most severe injury ever on the waterfront when he fractured his left leg while colliding with Yankees catcher Norman Kies on March 28, 1934. So upsetting was the injury that the game was not resumed. *Courtesy of the Library of Congress.*

attended to his leg at home plate, the imperturbable Rabbit smoked a cigarette. The crowd watched in silence as he was carted off to Mound Park Hospital in St. Pete, where he stayed until April 28. Rabbit did not return that season and played in only 23 games in 1935 before retiring.

7

FAREWELL

Babe Ruth sat in the dugout before what would be his last game at Yankee Stadium, a September Monday afternoon match against the Red Sox. It was not officially recognized as such, but the New York sportswriters had made it clear they thought it would be his last game as a regular. "Ruth will be with the Yankees again next season," wrote Dan Daniel in *The Sporting News*, "playing when he feels like it and pinch-hitting and coaching." The baseball writers of New York wanted to stage a Babe Ruth Day, but according to Daniel, "the Bam begged off, as he felt the fans would regard it as his departure from baseball."

It was the last home game of the 1934 season, and the Yankees entered play five and a half games behind the first-place Tigers with six to play. The crowd of 1,500, the smallest of the season, was strangely quiet. Paul Gallico of the *New York Daily News* described Yankee Stadium as a "yawning cavern." Gallico added:

> *Babe was glum and depressed. His final appearance had been extensively advertised. All of the papers carried it. Somehow, we all thought there would be an outpouring of the faithful to say "auf wiedersehen," if not "goodbye" to baseball's greatest figure. But there wasn't.*
>
> *I hadn't thought it possible for the crowds to forget quite so quickly. I know the Babe was deeply hurt. He gnawed off a corner of an oblong piece of tobacco, his fingers, as usual, ink-stained from autographing baseballs.*

He said in his rare and juicy vocabulary there was no fun in playing before a small crowd, but he would start the game. [Ruth started, but after walking in his first plate appearance, he pulled himself out due to a lingering "charley horse."] *We talked about the future. The Babe was very low in his mind. He said he felt like quitting.*

Ruth also made it clear that if he didn't receive an offer to manage, he was through.

Soon after the season, Ruth met with Yankees owner Colonel Jacob Ruppert, essentially seeking to replace manager Joe McCarthy. The headline on the front page of the October 18 *Sporting News* accurately summarized the meeting: "Ruth Shoots at McCarthy's Job, but Misses and Quits Yankees."

As Leigh Montville penned in his book *The Big Bam*, Ruth was now "a man without a country." And as the off-season wore on, there were only a couple of offers thrown his way, including one from a circus requiring the Babe to ride an elephant. The other was from the Boston Braves' owner, Judge Emil Fuchs, who offered Ruth a $25,000 salary, a cut of $10,000, a position as an executive vice-president with the team and an unusual position as assistant manager of the team, perhaps the early ancestor of today's bench coach. Fuchs's intentions were not well disguised. The Braves had finished twelfth out of sixteen teams in attendance in 1934.

The waning interest was not a complete surprise, as it paralleled the decline in Ruth's home run totals for each of his previous five seasons, culminating with 22 in 1934, his lowest total since 1925. He missed the first forty-one games of that season after he was stricken with the "bellyache heard 'round the world" in Asheville, North Carolina, onboard the Yankees' post–spring training, northbound team train.

With the clear intention of taking over for Braves manager Bill McKechnie—who would manage the team for the next three seasons and be elected to the Hall of Fame as a manager in 1962—Ruth signed with Boston, the Yankees' spring training cousins, on February 26.

On March 4, almost ten years to the day that the Babe first arrived in St. Petersburg amid great fanfare, Ruth stepped off the 5:00 p.m. Orange Blossom Special at the Seaboard Air Line train depot to an even greater reception, described in the *St. Petersburg Times* as the "most enthusiastic ever given a baseball player here." McKechnie and Al Lang were among the swarm estimated at three thousand, many of whom were there an hour before the train's arrival. It was reported that at every stop the train made in Florida, impromptu receptions broke out to honor the home run king.

Thousands of cheering fans greeted Babe Ruth (*center*) at the Seaboard Airline train station in St. Petersburg in the spring of 1935, his first with the Braves and the last of his career. Tampa Bay Times *photo*.

Pete Norton of the *Times* described it this way:

> *Any doubt that Babe Ruth is still the idol of young America was dispelled yesterday afternoon when the mighty Bambino arrived. Long before Ruth's train was scheduled to arrive here swarms of youngsters from eight years of age to 18 were milling around the railway station. Well-dressed kids from well-to-do families mingled with ragged urchins and chummed with the just average youngsters along the tracks, on top of box cars, and in every nook and cranny of the Seaboard station. Many of them had never seen the Babe before. Some were back for another look.*
>
> *It was a thrilling welcome to America's number one baseball hero and if we are any judge of human nature, the Babe was sincerely happy as he stepped from the train that had borne him from the north. The Babe, clad in a heavy winter suit, let loose with a big "Hello" as he stepped from the train to be immediately engulfed in a surging sea of humanity....Big drops of perspiration quickly formed on the Babe's smiling face as he tried to do a dozen things for the accommodation of photographers, newspapermen and his friends—the kids.*

It took a police escort to get Ruth and his wife to their car before making their way to their spring home at 346 Sixteenth Avenue Northeast.

"The coming of Babe Ruth as a member of the Boston Braves club was a signal for one of the greatest outpourings of stories with St. Petersburg datelines in the history of this city," Al Lang told the business community at a luncheon the next day, while Ruth was going through his first practice at the waterfront. Lang also announced that he had already received a dozen requests for Ruth to appear.

His dominance with the Braves was evident right from his first at bat at Waterfront Park. Ruth grumbled about the hitters' background, and immediately it was changed, according to author Kevin McCarthy in his book *Babe Ruth in Florida*. "The park had always provided a background of palm trees waving above the short centerfield fence," wrote McCarthy. "After Ruth complained, carpenters quickly set about tripling the height of the barriers giving it a more solid background."

A crowd estimated to be three thousand arrived an hour before the start of Babe's first workout with the Braves, scheduled for 11:00 a.m. on March 5 at Waterfront Park. The Yankees' camp, a scant two miles away, was unusually still as the New York media eschewed the team's workout for Ruth's debut. He didn't disappoint, hitting the second pitch he saw well over the fence in right while wearing a uniform borrowed from Yankees coach Hank Gowdy, as his had not yet arrived. That afternoon, Ruth shot an 82 at Pasadena Golf Club.

On March 16, a crowd of 4,726 watched the Braves and Yankees kick off the 1935 Grapefruit League season as St. Petersburg celebrated another record-breaking tourist season. Many were there to see Babe Ruth's first game against his former Yankees teammates; he singled in 3 at bats. Approximately 75,000 words were filed on telegraph lines around the world describing Ruth's first game against his former mates. Four days later, it was Dizzy Dean (HOF 1953) versus Babe Ruth that helped bring a record crowd of 6,467 to the waterfront. The Cards beat the Babe's Braves, 5–4. The crowd shattered the existing city record by 1,741.

"It was said that the population of St. Petersburg tripled when Ruth was playing baseball there," wrote Will Michaels in *The Making of St. Petersburg*. For Ruth, however, the euphoria of that spring didn't last long. The Babe batted only .156 (5-for-32), with no extra-base hits, at Waterfront Park. Ironically, in his last game there, it was a defensive play that marked the day. Ruth was the Braves' first baseman on a rare 5-2-3 triple play in a 7–5 loss to the Yankees. While Ruth was 0-for-1 with a walk, his Yankees replacement, George Selkirk, hit a 2-run double that brought home the tying and winning runs.

The Braves, however, were able to turn a profit during the spring for the first time in their history, and according to the March 22 edition of the *St. Petersburg Times*, the revenue was enough to pay all of their spring expenses and Ruth's salary for the coming season. It was not hyperbole when Al Lang remarked, "The Yankees with Babe Ruth and their stars meant millions to this town."

Sadly, after two months of the regular season, Ruth's unparalleled twenty-two-year playing career was over after batting just .181 in twenty-eight games with the Braves.

St. Petersburg lost not only the game's greatest player as a regular spring visitor but also one of its greatest philanthropists. Before leaving on the team train headed north from St. Petersburg for the last time, Ruth stopped by a high school senior cooking class to receive a chocolate cake as a thank-you gift. It would be impossible to calculate his philanthropic impact on the city and the joy he brought to the city's youth. Among his many fundraising efforts was his work toward establishing the Crippled Children's Hospital, renamed Johns Hopkins All Children's Hospital in 1967.

When Larry MacPhail joined the Brooklyn Dodgers as general manager in 1938, he was acutely aware of the need to increase attendance. The previous year, the New York Giants had led the senior circuit with crowds almost twice that of the Dodgers' total of 482,481. Accordingly, MacPhail convinced Ruth to join the team as a coach. Attendance increased by more than 20,000 at Ruth's return, but, at the end of the season, when the Dodgers hired Leo Durocher to manage the team, Ruth resigned, ending his association with Major League Baseball. Many years later, first baseman Dolph Camilli, who joined the Dodgers that season, said of Ruth: "He was the most likable of guys. He was just himself, the Babe, the one and only. The best ever. Take my word for it; he would have been a successful manager had he been given the chance."

Author McCarthy described Ruth's relationship with the Sunshine State this way:

> Both parties, the ballplayer and the state prospered from encounters with each other. As a Yankee and a Brave, he spent many springs there to get his body into shape, show his employers that he was still able to hit the long ball and enthrall a public that never got its fill of the man. Florida likewise gained from his presence not only in the increase in the number of tourists

who flocked to the state each March to watch the boys of summer, but also from the ballplayers who returned there after their careers were over, from the millions of words written from the Sunshine State and from the high praise that Ruth always had for the state....Florida and Babe Ruth came of age together.

• • • •

March 17, 1936
Joe DiMaggio played his first game in a Yankee uniform and was 4-for-5 with a triple in an 8–7 loss to the Cardinals in the Yankees' home opener. In his second game on the Waterfront, two days later, DiMaggio recorded 4 singles in a 13–8 win over the Reds. Lefty Gomez (HOF 1972) worked three hitless, scoreless innings for the win while overcoming 7 walks.

March 21, 1936
In his third home game, DiMaggio singled in his first 2 at bats, giving him 10 hits in his first 13 at bats in St. Pete, but Braves second baseman Joe Coscarart accidentally stepped on Joe DiMaggio's left ankle, and things went from bad to worse. While being treated for the injury, Yankees trainer Doc Earle Painter kept Joe's foot in the diathermy machine too long, and he suffered second-degree burns. DiMaggio would miss the remainder of the spring schedule and the first eighteen games of the regular season.

March 16, 1937
Mel Ott (HOF 1951) hit a 3-run home run, highlighting a 6-run fifth inning, and Vince DiMaggio, brother of Joe, hit his first homer in a major league uniform as the New York Giants beat the Braves, 8–6. Ott went on to hit a National League–high 31, the fourth of six times the five-foot, nine-inch twelve-time All-Star would lead the senior circuit.

8

A SIXTY-YEAR ROMANCE

Like seemingly everything else in Florida good or bad, the breakup between St. Petersburg and the Boston Bees (the team went by "Bees" between 1936 and 1940) had something to do with the weather. The relationship began crumbling in 1936, when the first two games of the season, a weekend series between the Bees and the Yankees, were rained out. It was the second of those games that got under the skin of Bees president Bob Quinn, who complained that the game could have been played if "a little more attention had been paid to muck from the diamond." Quinn took his beef to the chamber of commerce, but the bad feelings lingered over the following two springs, until July 12, 1937, when Quinn informed the media—not the city or Al Lang—that they would not be returning to St. Petersburg, ending a sixteen-year affiliation.

That was on Tuesday. By Saturday, Lang had secured a new tenant. And not just any tenant. The St. Louis Cardinals—the famed Gashouse Gang—agreed to leave Daytona Beach for the Sunshine City. While the incumbent Yankees had the best record in the American League over the previous twelve seasons, the Cardinals owned the National League's best mark over that same span. St. Petersburg now had them both, and the two would play each other 117 times on the waterfront grounds over the next six decades. It was a one-year deal, but Cardinals president Sam Breadon stated that he expected the Cardinals to remain indefinitely. In this case, indefinitely meant until 1997. Prior to one of the ensuing spring openers

Stan Musial (*left*) and Al Lang (*right*) water the infield at Waterfront Park prior to World War II. *Courtesy of St. Petersburg Museum of History.*

between the two teams, Lonnie Burtt of the *St. Petersburg Times* playfully wrote, "Florida's greatest attraction equaled only by the sunshine and grapefruit, goes on today as the New York Yankees and St. Louis Cardinals slice open the Grapefruit League season."

Having both heralded teams sharing the same field only solidified St. Pete as the spring baseball capital. *St Petersburg Times* sports editor Jack Ellison wrote in the spring of 1955, "There are so many datelines appearing in the nation's press these days that I hear the Reds are kicking themselves for changing the name of that city from St. Petersburg to Stalingrad."

Lang had tried valiantly to keep the Braves satisfied while they played in the game's largest shadow. "Baseball," he said, "has been the making of St. Petersburg.

I believe that the coming of the Yankees and Braves to our city each winter has been as great a factor for attracting people here as any other single attribute we have. Before the Braves started training here our tourist population was almost exclusively from the Midwest. The first year the Braves trained in St. Petersburg marked a 40 percent increase in New England tourism registrations. The decision of the Yankees to come to St. Petersburg increased the number of winter registrations from New York by 200 percent. The millions of words of favorable publicity from this city each year by sportswriters covering the camps are read each year by millions of readers all over this country and Canada. Now with the Yankees and Cardinals we have this ideal set up.

At the time and for the next seventeen years, the Cardinals were major league baseball's westernmost city. And when KMOX Radio signed on in 1926, their reach was unmatched. As former Cardinals catcher Tim McCarver noted in his book *Few and Chosen*: "The entire South, Southwest and much of the West was saturated with Cardinals baseball. As a result, next to the Yankees, the Cardinals were arguably the most popular team in the country. Not as rabid as the Dodgers following, but popular."

It wasn't always harmonious, according to several reports in the *St. Petersburg Times*. In 1946, Yankees president Larry MacPhail angrily forced the Cardinals to cancel a doubleheader versus the Reds when he claimed he should have been informed in advance of the twin bill. The Yankees were scheduled to play the Reds the next day. He also pressured the Cards to change their game times from 2:00 p.m. (the standard times for all Grapefruit League games) by thirty minutes to accommodate a request from a radio station. And, in 1954, there was a dustup between the two organizations over shared parking and practice times.

There was also instant tension between Lang and Cardinals president Fred Saigh, who had purchased the team from Breadon in 1947. Within two years, Lang wanted to make a change and bring the big-market Braves back to St. Petersburg. Armed with the tourist registration figures to prove that the city received more business from Massachusetts than Missouri, Lang told *The Sporting News*: "I'm trying to do what's best for St. Petersburg. It's strictly business with me. If I went by sentiment, I would have the Pirates from my native Pittsburgh and Connie Mack's Athletics here."

But in September 1949, with Lang and a pro-Lang councilman out of town, the city council voted to extend the Cardinals' lease for ten years. Lang was devastated when he learned of the news. Saigh, however, never made it through the lease. Convicted of income-tax evasion, he sold the Cards to August Busch and his St. Louis brewery interests. Lang and Busch soon became allies.

The Cardinals' inaugural workout came on March 2, 1938, at Waterfront Park, and Manager Frankie Frisch led the group while hobbling about on crutches, the result of a foot fracture he suffered at the team's winter school in Winter Haven ten days before. The *St. Petersburg Times* observed, "While what was said to be the largest crowd ever to watch the opening of a major league baseball camp roared its approval, Frisch spark-plugged his Red Birds in a short morning workout and then called them out again in the afternoon for an hour and a half session." Al Lang and the team's brass were

Cardinals engage in sliding practice at Al Lang. *Courtesy of St. Petersburg Museum of History.*

Julian Javier is the St. Louis base runner, and Joe Pepitone is at first base for the Yankees in the Cards' win over the Yankees in 1966, 1 of 138 meetings between the two teams on the waterfront. *Courtesy of St. Petersburg Museum of History.*

there; Ducky Medwick, the team's future Hall of Fame outfielder, was not. Embroiled in a contract dispute, he was attending the opening round of the St. Petersburg Open Golf Tournament.

In their first game as the home team on the waterfront on March 12, 1938, the Cardinals played the Yankees. The game drew a city record of 6,948 spectators. The Yankees won, 6–4, despite playing without future Hall of Famers Lou Gehrig, Joe DiMaggio and Bill Terry. It was another future Hall of Famer, Joe Gordon, a rookie playing in his first game in a Yankees uniform, who delivered a bases-loaded triple in a 6-run sixth inning. The next day, the Cards used a rare 7-run tenth inning to dispose of the Yankees, 8–1.

The St. Louis organization and its players took to their new surroundings quickly. After earning a 3–0 win over the Dodgers on the last day of March, the Cards' sixteen-game winner Lefty Weiland and other teammates who were members of the Mudcat Band—the team's roguish leader, Pepper Martin's, outfit—played square-dancing music at the Golden Jubilee

Spectacle in downtown St. Pete as part of the celebration surrounding the city's annual Festival of States parade. The ragtag band performed the next night as well and was a regular at events around the city, including informally in the outdoor lobby of the team's host, the Detroit Hotel. The group featured Martin and Lon Warneke on guitar, Weiland on the jug, Max Lanier on the harmonica, Frenchy Bordagaray on the washboard and thimbles and Bill McGee on the violin. "Buffalo Gal" was the band's favorite. They often rehearsed on the team's cross-country train rides.

The week before, the Cardinals invited all St. Petersburg youngsters between the ages of ten and sixteen to attend their game with the Tigers for free, a first for the city. A season-high paid crowd of 4,274 was swelled even greater by the presence of the Cards' guests. After the game, the St. Petersburg Chamber of Commerce held a dinner at the Princess Martha as the city's way of showing appreciation for both teams, the first such dinner ever held in the Sunshine City.

On the last day of the 1938 spring season, the *St. Petersburg Times* described the value of having the Yankees and Cardinals at Waterfront Park as "inestimable." And Cardinals manager and future Hall of Famer Frankie Frisch said without hesitation: "This has certainly been the ideal spot with great interest from the fans, a perfect break in the weather, plenty of clubhouse facilities. We trimmed the Yankees four games to two in the St. Petersburg city series, and if you ask me, that is just about what we will take them next Fall in the [World] Series."

It didn't quite turn out that way. The Yankees beat the Cubs in the Fall Classic; the Cardinals finished sixth in the National League.

• • • •

March 20, 1938
Lefty Gomez (HOF 1972) and Red Ruffing (HOF 1967) combined on a 3-hit, 1–0 win over St. Louis' Gashouse Gang. Lou Gehrig's (HOF 1939) first-inning single drove in the game's lone run.

March 22, 1938
The Yankees beat the Dodgers, 7–0, as Hall of Fame catcher Bill Dickey singled, doubled and tripled. Lou Gehrig was hitless, but before the game at the Yankees' facility at Huggins Field, he rode a western steed across the diamond and lassoed several teammates as part of the promotion for his upcoming movie, *Rawhide*, which

would debut at St. Petersburg's Capitol Theatre that night. The page-one review of the movie written by *St. Petersburg Times* critic Jack Thale included this: "From a technical standpoint, Lou may never win an academy award for his acting, but according to the picture last night, he is far from being the worst actor that ever trod the boards." Exactly one year and one week later, Whitney Martin of the Associated Press wrote a different critique entirely: "They are saying loudly now that the Iron has rusted; that the marvelous physical machine that carried Lou Gehrig through 2,122 consecutive games has fallen apart; that the streak will surely end this year."

March 27, 1938
The Yankees dropped a 10–3 decision to Dizzy Dean (HOF 1953) and their city mate Cardinals. The victory clinched the season set for the Gashouse Gang, four games to two. Cardinals farmhand shortstop Sammy Baugh, who the previous fall had led the Washington Redskins to the National Football League championship as a rookie quarterback, had 2 hits and 2 RBIs. Baugh, who was inducted into the Pro Football Hall of Fame in 1963 after a sixteen-year career with the Redskins, played only one season of pro baseball, appearing in fifty-three games combined in the International League and American Association.

March 21, 1939
The Tigers' stars roared to life as they defeated the Cardinals, 7–3. Second baseman Charlie Gehringer (HOF 1949) had 2 hits; first baseman Hank Greenberg (HOF 1956), the AL's reigning home run champ, homered and singled; and seven-time All-Star catcher Rudy York had an RBI single

March 20, 1940
Twenty-one-year-old Ted Williams (HOF 1966) ripped a 440-foot inside-the-park home run, a drive that careened off a palm tree inside the fence in center field, giving the Red Sox a 1–0 win over the Cardinals. He barely beat the relay throw to the plate. Williams added 2 singles and three fine defensive catches in left field.

March 6, 1942
In his first game at Waterfront Park, Stan Musial singled, doubled and homered against the Yankees in an 8–7, ten-inning loss. The two teams played nine times that spring (the Cardinals won the series, six games to three) and then faced each other in the World Series.

March 20, 1942
After a ten-year career with the Pirates, Arky Vaughan (HOF 1985) was traded to the Dodgers. In his Waterfront Park debut, he went 4-for-6 with 4 RBIs in a 12–4 win over the Yankees in a battle of defending league champions.

March 27, 1942
Vince DiMaggio got 3 hits for Boston, and brother Joe added 2 for the Yankees, in their battle at Waterfront Park. The Yankees prevailed, 3–2, by scoring 2 runs in the bottom of the thirteenth, the winning run scoring on Bill Dickey's sharp walk-off single down the third-base line.

9

WAR!

Despite the death sentence Al Lang was handed years before, the *New York Times'* Arthur Daley wrote: "The closest he ever came to dying was when wartime restrictions forced the teams to train in the frozen North. That almost broke Al's heart."

The Sporting News called him a "war orphan." In a letter to the *Cincinnati Post's* Tom Swope, Lang himself admitted: "I'm like a fish out of water. This will be the first spring since 1914 that I have not had my gang around me at St. Petersburg and I am certainly going to miss the bunch." Lang was referring to team employees, officials, players, fans and, of course, the writers.

It might be that Lang's passion for baseball and St. Petersburg was never more evident than when there was no baseball. The United States was at war in Europe and the Pacific when, on December 22, 1942, the Cardinals and Yankees canceled spring training in St. Petersburg, snapping a string of twenty-one consecutive years of Major League Baseball on the waterfront. A month later, baseball commissioner Kenesaw Mountain Landis made it official for all clubs: due to wartime travel restrictions, major league teams would have to train north of the Potomac and Ohio Rivers for the upcoming season, with the exception of the Cardinals and Browns, who were given the option of using Missouri as a site. The Yankees trained at Asbury Park High School in Asbury Park, New Jersey, in 1943 and at Bader Field in Atlantic City in 1944 and 1945. The Cards trained at Cotter Field in Cairo, Illinois, in 1943 and 1944 but retreated to Sportsman's Park in St. Louis in 1945, when flooding made the Cairo field unplayable. The ban would last three years, the only period in which St. Petersburg was without Major League Baseball between 1922 and 2008. Landis's announcement came on the same day the U.S. government purchased one of the city's jewels, the Don DeSar Hotel on St. Pete Beach, for $440,000. It would serve as a military hospital during the war and wouldn't return to hotel status until 1973.

Lang was politically correct in saying: "If it will help win the war, we can graciously surrender our teams. Naturally it will be a disappointment to the soldiers who have never seen major league baseball and were anxious to see both teams in action. But winning the war comes first and we're more than willing to do everything possible. But I want to assure everyone that we will have our teams back as soon as the war is over."

It didn't take long, however, for his restlessness to take over. A few months after Florida's first spring without baseball, or about the same time the Allies took Sicily, Lang launched his own offensive. "The (military) boys in training in our state have begged for major league baseball," he told *The Sporting News* before he went off to plead his case to government, team and league officials to lift the travel restrictions.

Wouldn't it be better, he asked the commissioner, if baseball brought spring training back to Florida the following spring as a means to entertain the troops? *The Sporting News* in its April 1, 1943 edition agreed:

> *The average soldier is so much more interested in Charlie Keller or Morton Cooper than he is in a touring radio commentator or lecturer. On their day off, Sunday, hundreds roam the streets with nothing else to do. What a treat it would have been for these boys if the Yankees and Cardinals had spent their usual five weekends at Waterfront Park, playing over the World Series as well as meeting the Red Sox, Reds, Tigers, Indians and other clubs which in the past had trained within a fifty-mile radius of St. Petersburg. So hungry were the soldiers for a sight of big leaguers that when the three Yankee pitchers Johnny Murphy, Atlee Donald and Spud Chandler worked out for a couple of weeks, the little stands at Miller Huggins were full of men in khaki, soldiers on leave or enjoying a day off.*

On the other hand, while there was no major league spring baseball or minor league baseball being played on the waterfront, the field was far from neglected. The war actually brought more people to the Sunshine City. The army had established a training center in St. Petersburg. According

Military drills took place on many of St. Pete's waterfront parks during World War II, including at Vinoy Park (*pictured*) and Waterfront Park. *Courtesy of St. Petersburg Museum of History.*

to *St. Petersburg and Its People*, a total of 119,057 military personnel passed through the city during the war years. Between military softball, baseball and boxing, Waterfront Park was alive most afternoons. It was another activity that may have caused the most harm to the beloved turf. "The army has used it for drilling purposes, and the outfield in which Babe Ruth once held forth has been churned into black dust," *The Sporting News* reported on March 18, 1943. In September, the City of St. Petersburg ordered reconditioning of Al Lang Field in anticipation of the return of major league spring training in 1944. Who would doubt Lang didn't have a hand in such legislation?

It would be two more years before the wartime travel plan was lifted, but before it was, Lang issued an invitation to big league clubs to send players to St. Pete for pre–training camp activities. He even planned for American League clubs to use the Huggins site and National Leaguers to work out at Waterfront Park.

Finally, on August 17, 1945, the Office of Defense Transportation lifted the sports travel ban. The Cardinals and Yankees would begin spring workouts at Waterfront Park on Monday, February 18. The Yankees would get a head start with a pre–spring training eleven-game tour in Panama.

A little more than a month after the announcement, Lang invited discharged major league veterans to St. Petersburg to train at Al Lang. He also promised them residential accommodations in keeping within their means. No less than A's president and manager Connie Mack endorsed the plan. Lang told *The Sporting News*:

> *Hundreds of players who played no baseball at all while they were in the Army, Navy, Marines and Coast Guard are coming back. We think we can help such players get back into their old baseball form. Besides there will be some players who have to get the feel of baseball again. Our thought is to start these players with sports which are exercises as well as recreational activities. If they want to do any light throwing, Waterfront Park, with its clubhouse and showers will be available. Then as the actual baseball training season approaches, these players can accelerate their training. In that way we think we can turn over some pretty well conditioned players to their various team by the end of February.*

Among the players who took him up on it was Phillies pitcher Jim Mulcahy, who was the first big league player to enter the service during the war, doing so in the spring of 1941. He returned in late summer of 1945 and appeared in five games for Philadelphia. He was woefully out of shape and in the off-season took his wife and newborn son and headed to St. Petersburg to begin a training regimen in preparation for the Phillies' training camp at Miami Beach. "It's really something to be able to get out on the winding roads along the shore, whenever circling the course around Waterfront gets tiresome," Mulcahy told *The Sporting News*. "It's putting my legs in the shape needed to carry me through my first full big league schedule in six years." Before the war, his claim to fame was leading the National League in losses in 1938 and 1940 and still making the All-Star team in the latter season. He pitched parts of 1946 and 1947 before retiring.

The headline in the March 7, 1946 edition of *The Sporting News* proclaimed "Sunny St. Pete Back on Big Time Beat and City Rejoices over Return of Yanks and Cardinals after Absence of Three Years." And, "St. Petersburg Proudly Calls Itself the 'Twelfth Major League City.'" The annual spring migration of national media from the North had begun, and they may have outnumbered the Canadian geese. Dan Hall, columnist for the *St. Petersburg Times*, observed, "Al Lang is quietly going mad trying to find hotel reservations for all the nationally prominent sports writers and radio commentators who want to come here for spring training season."

A B-36 bomber flies over Al Lang Field and the West Coast Inn, where Babe Ruth's legendary home run struck the second floor in 1934. *Courtesy of St. Petersburg Museum of History.*

Returning to St. Petersburg after a three-year break, veteran baseball writer Dan Daniel wrote in the third person on March 7:

> *Your correspondent has seen every training locale in this country. He has seen all the camps from Charlottesville, Va., where the Senators worked out years ago, before the war, to Catalina Island. And it is his conviction that St. Petersburg is the best of the lot. For winter alone, dry San Antonio takes the palm. But for all around superiority, St. Pete is tops. In St. Petersburg, you draw a crowd for every workout and you are sure of a good house for every game. Hotels are fine, and municipal appreciation for the good a ballclub does for a town is high, thanks in large measure, to Al Lang.*

It wasn't all perfect. St. Petersburg's omnipresent sand often made Waterfront Park's footing a bit tricky, but after years as a military drill ground, it had reached a new low. Cardinals manager Eddie Dyer complained about the "sand traps" in the outfield that had led to a number of leg injuries. After arriving at the Cards' 1946 camp a bit late due to his military commitment, Stan Musial promptly slipped while playing pepper on the field and stretched ligaments in his left knee, further setting back his training. In one of the last games of the 1946 spring season, Musial again took a tumble on one of those sand traps but escaped injury. And in early March, center fielder Terry Moore missed two weeks with an injury after taking a misstep on the uneven surface. Also unsafe was the park's old wooden grandstands, where small fires brought about by careless smokers were not uncommon.

The most disappointed group may have been the wives of the players, staff and writers. Postwar team rosters swelled to seventy-five players or more, creating a housing shortage and forcing all of the Florida teams to prohibit players from bringing their families to spring training. The Cardinals' hotel, the Bainbridge, and the Yankees' headquarters at the Suwanee were filled to capacity.

But baseball was back. On March 9, three years, eleven months and four days since the last Grapefruit League was played on the waterfront, the Yankees beat the Cardinals, 5–0, in front of 5,385 happy fans. Future Hall of Famer Joe Gordon hit a 3-run home run, and three Yankees pitchers limited the Redbirds to 3 hits. By spring's end, a city-record 55,039 spectators had watched baseball at the worn, wooden stadium. Scouts, too, were on hand in big numbers to see the postwar Yankees and Cardinals in what would be Waterfront Park's last season. Twelve of the sixteen clubs were represented.

The Cardinals in one of the last games at Waterfront Park. *Courtesy of St. Petersburg Museum of History.*

On top of that, fourteen of the sixteen major league teams were now training in Florida. But one more question still needed to be answered. "Why does a city that draws 55,000 to see training games," the skeptical Dyer posed to the *St. Petersburg Times*, "put up with a grandstand like that?"

• • • •

March 19, 1946
Joe DiMaggio hit his fifth home run in seven games at Waterfront Park that spring, but the Cardinals won on a two-out, 2-run home run by pinch-hitter Walter Sessi, an ex-army officer who had just returned from military duty after missing four seasons.

March 22, 1946
The Tigers beat the Yankees despite the hitting of Joe DiMaggio, who hit 2 home runs, and Charlie Keller, who hit the longest home

run of the season at Waterfront Park. DiMaggio finished with 7 home runs in 12 home games and added 6 more on the road, by far his best spring.

March 31, 1946

With Bob Feller starting for the Indians, Waterfront Park saw a Sunday record 3,716 fans in the seats. Feller pitched seven innings, allowing 2 runs while striking out 7. The Cardinals won, 3–2, in ten innings on rookie first baseman Dick Sisler's single.

10

AL LANG FIELD...FINALLY

Al Lang received the best seventy-fifth birthday present he could ever hope for when, at the St. Pete City Council on November 16, 1945, he was presented with a resolution to name a new baseball stadium Albert F. Lang Field. Construction was to begin after the 1946 Grapefruit League season. The proclamation read: "Whereas it is the opinion of this council that Albert Fielding Lang has done more than any other citizen of this city to encourage, foster and develop major league baseball in this community be it resolved by the city council and the City of St. Petersburg, that the proposed baseball field and recreation field to be constructed immediately, a block south of the present waterfront ball park site be designated Albert F. Lang Field."

This was a birthday present earned, not merely given, and it ended years of Lang's hard work to bring his city a much-needed ballpark. As far back as 1925, weeks after the Yankees had completed their first spring in St. Petersburg, James Coad, the executive vice-president of the St. Petersburg Chamber of Commerce, stated to the *St. Petersburg Times*: "Speaking for myself, I would like nothing better than to see a great stadium built on the site of Waterfront Park, the name to be Lang Stadium. It would be a fitting expression of our appreciation for Al Lang." In 1928, American League President E.S. Barnard said at a St. Petersburg Rotary meeting that, while the city was in no danger of losing its teams, it needed a larger stadium to accommodate crowds that were as large as those that attend major league games in the big league cities themselves.

Al Lang Field. *Courtesy of Florida Memory, the State Library and Archives of Florida.*

But the stadium issue lingered. The wooden grandstand at Waterfront Park had been plagued by eleven small fires in the bleachers in 1939 alone. While everyone agreed a new ballpark was needed, there was no consensus as to where it should be built. At a hearing held by the city's chamber of commerce in the spring of 1939, Paul R. Boardman, the meeting's first speaker, stated, "We have a beautiful waterfront, but it should be made more beautiful by removing the ballpark."

Parking, too, was an issue. "Many people are being driven away from the games. They won't bother driving around and around looking for a parking space," declared Councilman George W. Hopkins. Finally, at a city council meeting on May 23, 1939, after interminable debate, it was agreed to locate a permanent baseball stadium in Woodlawn Park at Sixteenth Street and Thirteenth Avenue North. The new proposed stadium would be ready in time for the 1940 spring training season. The city's waterfront preservationists had lobbied for the park to be moved, so the day was a momentary victory for them. Not for Lang, and not for long.

"To change the location to Woodlawn Park would make the park inaccessible, would involve an immense outlay of money by the city and require a bonus of $10,000 to the Cardinals and about $15,000 to the Yankees," Lang rebutted, according to the *St. Petersburg Times*. While Lang much preferred the waterfront location, his primary concern, as always, was keeping the teams happy.

Construction at Woodlawn was scheduled to start on two separate occasions in 1939, but ten months later, the project still had not gotten off the ground. Finance challenges and opposition to the move from various groups, including the downtown hoteliers, thwarted the city's efforts. There was even a petition signed by sixty-seven guests of the Soreno Hotel.

Meanwhile, the city regarded as the best spring training location in Florida missed out on an opportunity to host a one-time event: a Major League All-Star Game for charity in the spring of 1940. "St. Petersburg has lost this priceless publicity opportunity because we haven't got a decent ballpark for the game to be played in," Lang was quoted as saying at the time in the *St. Petersburg Times*. "It breaks my heart for St. Petersburg to sit idly by and let golden opportunities slip through their fingers like this." (Thirteen future Hall of Famers, only four fewer than played in the annual All-Star Game at Sportsman's Park in St. Louis that July, played in the game at Tampa's Plant Field on March 17. The exhibition drew more than thirteen thousand spectators while raising approximately $20,000 for the people of Finland, who had been attacked by the Soviet Union in December 1939.) Tampa's favorite son and future Hall of Fame catcher Al Lopez scored the winning run.

So, when the Cardinals arrived that spring, there was no ballpark. "When they left last March, they expected to find a waterfront park with a modern grandstand seating at least 5,000 when they returned," said an irritated Lang, according to the *Times*.

Cardinals owner Sam Breadon added that although the team had no intention of leaving St. Petersburg, "Having the Cardinals and Yankees play at antiquated Waterfront Park was like staging the Zigfeld Follies in a nickelodian." At a press conference on March 25, officials from the Yankees and the Cardinals voiced their opposition to suggestions of moving off the waterfront, effectively killing the Woodlawn plan. According to the *Times*, Cardinals owner Sam Breadon told city officials, "The waterfront location makes St. Petersburg the biggest baseball city in Florida. You will flirt with disaster if you move it—it's one of your biggest attractions." The Yankees' president Ed Barrow agreed, adding that a large part of the attendance during the training season is elderly people. "We lose them if the park is moved," he contended, "so why not develop the present waterfront site?"

While World War II would further delay the process, the good news was that it was finally agreed by most that a new waterfront park was needed, and that idea finally began to crystallize over Lang's birthday cake.

Not yet at the finish line, a small group of citizens had already tried suing the city, claiming that the spring training games and amateur nighttime softball leagues (illuminated by floodlights) at Waterfront Park were a nuisance. On May 27, 1942, the Pinellas Circuit Court denied the arguments of the anti-ballpark group, but protest groups remained active on the waterfront, according to the *Times*, even during the 1946 season.

There was also the matter of the Office of Price Administration's ban on any new U.S. construction other than for war veterans. The housing embargo essentially dissolved that summer, but construction didn't begin until May 27, nearly two months after Lang had hoped for and nine months before the park's scheduled opening in March 1947. The entire operation was put at risk on June 26, when it appeared the necessary steel for the grandstand would not be delivered on time. Ingalls Steel of Birmingham, Alabama, reported that it would be unable to deliver its product as originally promised due to labor issues in the steel and coal industries. The panicky headline in the *Times* the next day moaned, "Steel for Grandstand Delayed; City May Lose Yankees, Cards." The next day, the city located and contracted with a Tampa company, Bushnell-Lyons, to have the steel delivered on time for $25,934, approximately $10,000 higher than the original bid

Al Lang Field, with Demens Landing and the pier in the background. *Courtesy of St. Petersburg Museum of History.*

On September 21, demolition began on the old grandstand, where a parking lot for five hundred cars would be paved. Work quickly began on the new grandstand, which would be located at the approximate site of second base at Waterfront Park.

Two weeks before Christmas, Lang gave a complete tour of the new park to Yankees president Larry MacPhail, who had nothing but praise for his team's new home. Lang, too, admitted it exceeded his expectations. During that visit, it was announced that the city would share in the gate receipts from the spring games for the first time. The arrangement would yield several thousand dollars annually to the city, keeping a promise both the Yankees and the Cardinals made as an incentive to build a new ballpark.

In February, the city's chamber of commerce took out a series of advertisements in *The Sporting News* inviting fans to "plan a vacation at baseball's winter capital," likely the first city to do so.

On March 12, 1947, the first game was played at the $300,000 concrete and steel park called "one of the finest in the nation" by *The Sporting News* in its March 19 edition. The park had 750 box seats and 3,800 general admission seats, while the bleachers accommodated another 3,000. Unlike its predecessor, the new park had seating with arm supports. Unlike the asymmetrical, cavernous Waterfront Park, Al Lang's dimensions would be a bit more reasonable measuring 309 feet down each foul line, 350 in the alleys and 397 to center. The infield was a mixture of imported Georgia clay and Florida sand. And Cards skipper Eddie Dyer got his fresh sod.

The first game between the park's two inhabitants—the soon-to-be 1947 world champion Yankees and the 1946 world champion Cardinals—drew a crowd of 7,706, the largest ever to see a game in St. Petersburg. Among the spectators were Commissioner Albert B. Chandler, American League president Will Harridge, dean of sportswriters Grantland Rice and the team presidents of both the Yankees and Cardinals. Lang was among those who spoke and asked for a moment of silence in memory of Lou Gehrig and famed New York sportswriter Sid Mercer.

Rice, recognized as that era's greatest sportswriter, wrote a poem for the occasion, the last stanza of which follows.

> *When Cain and Abel fought it out before an ancient mob,*
> *When no one ever heard of Ruth, of Speaker or of Cobb,*
> *When Cardinals were always last or even lower still,*
> *And Cat Brecheen was much too young to throw the winning pill,*
> *When Slaughter had no arm at all, with Musial and Moore,*

Al Lang was bringing Ivory to St. Pete's sunny shore.
So let's now all stand and sing that more than famous line,
"Should old acquaintance be forgot—three cheers for Auld Lang zyne."

And then came the game, which was carried live back to New York on WINS Radio, which for the first time would broadcast all Yankees home spring games. The Cardinals scored 6 runs in the bottom of the first inning and roughed up the Yankees, 10–5. Stan Musial hit the first home run, a sixth-inning, 400-foot blast off the Yankees' Randy Gumpert. The home run landed on First Street, some 400 feet from home plate and followed Cardinals outfielder Dick Sisler's ground-rule double, which rolled under the benches in center field. The game featured seven future Hall of Famers: Musial, Yogi Berra, Red Schoendienst, Phil Rizzuto, Joe Medwick, Enos Slaughter and Yankees manager Bucky Harris. It was Berra's first game on the waterfront, and he played right field, a trial that didn't last long before he was back behind the plate. On that day, though, he had 2 hits and an RBI and played errorless ball.

At the end of the greatest day in his storied life, a day that included a luncheon of visiting baseball dignitaries at the St. Petersburg Yacht Club, an onfield speech prior to the first pitch, the 2:30 p.m. game, endless meet and greets and an evening nationwide radio interview, Al Lang dragged himself back to his Beach Drive apartment and retired for the evening. Several hours later, he was awakened and unable to sleep, got up thinking that it must have been early morning. It was, in fact, 11:30 p.m. "You know," he told the *St. Petersburg Times*, "it was the first time in 20 years I had been to bed before 11:30 p.m."

The only drawbacks to the 1947 season were three rainouts that kept the teams from setting their all-time spring attendance record and a heel injury that kept Joe DiMaggio out all spring. But the new ballpark also spurred the return of something else. For the first time since 1928, when the Florida State League disbanded midseason, St. Petersburg would have minor league baseball. On November 15, 1946, the one-year-old, six-team Florida International League (FIL) granted franchises to St. Pete and Ft. Lauderdale. A month later, the city council granted the new Saints franchise a five-year lease and permission to install lights needed for the team to play 77 night games that summer. The lights would meet the standards for minor league baseball, not major league baseball.

Minor league baseball would continue in the Sunshine City for the next fifty-four years, fifty-three of those at Al Lang. The Saints won the 1951 FIL championship, and when the league folded in July 1954, they emerged as a new member of the Florida State League the following season.

The city also considered a proposal from the All-American Girls Professional Baseball League (AAGPBL) to place a franchise in St. Petersburg as part of a possible international winter league circuit being considered by AAGPBL commissioner Arthur Meyerhoff. Lang and the city's baseball committee turned down the request over worry that the winter league would leave Al Lang Field in poor condition for major league spring training. Forty-eight years later, Al Lang Stadium hosted the Pepsi XLs in the ill-fated eight-team Women's Baseball Association, which failed to complete its inaugural season in 1995.

• • • •

March 30, 1948
The first of three no-hitters thrown on the waterfront came courtesy of Murry Dickson, a relatively obscure, 155-pound Cardinals right-hander. Dickson blanked the Yankees, 7–0, while striking out 6, walking 5 and hitting one batter. The Cards helped him with three double plays. Dickson threw just the second nine-inning no-hitter in major league spring training history, joining Pittsburgh's Cy Blanton, who blanked the Cleveland Indians at New Orleans on April 9, 1939.

April 4, 1948
Ten days after his walk-off single beat the reigning World Series champion Yankees, 8–7, Stan Musial did it again. This time, it was 2-run, 425-foot walk-off homer that gave the Cardinals another 8–7 win, clinching the city championship, five games to four.

March 12, 1949
After having not managed in the big leagues since 1943, Casey Stengel returned for his first game in a Yankees uniform. In front of 6,854 fans, the second-largest crowd in St. Pete history, the Yankees thumped the Cardinals, 10–3.

April 6, 1949
At the age of eighty-six, Connie Mack, the longest-serving manager in major league history, helmed his last game on the waterfront,

twenty-two years after his first. Mack served as owner-manager of the Philadelphia A's for fifty-three years. Dick Fowler threw a complete game four-hitter as Mack's A's beat the Yankees, 6–1.

February 7, 1950
The great Joe Louis, who held the title of World Heavyweight Champion for more than eleven years, fought a four-round boxing exhibition with Nino Valdez at Al Lang Field before four thousand fans.

April 4, 1950
In what turned out to be his last game in St. Petersburg, Joe DiMaggio hit a 3-run homer off the Tigers' 19-game-winner, Virgil Trucks, in a 6–4 loss. The crowd of 3,132 brought the season total to more than 75,000 for the first time in the waterfront's history. The Tigers scored 3 runs in the eighth off losing pitcher Don Johnson, who was also the victim of a triple steal—Hall of Famer George Kell scored the run, and Hoot Evers and Johnny Groth swiped third and second, respectively.

January 14, 1951
In what is considered the largest crowd to ever attend an event at Al Lang, a gathering of somewhere between 15,000 and 20,000 was on hand on a Sunday afternoon to hear the Reverend Billy Graham speak. Ten years later, he returned and brought roughly the same number of people despite a cold, rainy day in January.

March 10, 1951
The New York Giants played their first game at Al Lang and their first in St. Petersburg since 1940, after the Giants and Yankees agreed to switch spring training homes for one year. The Yankees had moved to the Giants' camp in Arizona. The Cardinals won, 4–2, before 6,654. While the Giants featured one future Hall of Famer in left fielder Monte Irvin, another didn't appear in St. Petersburg that spring. Willie Mays, who would go on to hit 20 homers for the National League champions that season, spent the spring at Sanford, Florida, home of the Giants' minor league camp. Manager Leo Durocher did make a trip to Sanford to see the prized rookie and was not disappointed.

11

BREAKING BARRIERS

On March 13, 1950, three years after Jackie Robinson broke Major League Baseball's color barrier but two years before Robinson would make his Al Lang debut, Boston Braves outfielder Sam Jethroe became the first Black major leaguer to play on the waterfront. Unlike the throngs that would greet Robinson, no one seemed to notice. There was only one mention of Jethroe in the following day's *St. Petersburg Times* other than the box score. It was a brief note suggesting that now that the color barrier had been broken at Al Lang, maybe the Dodgers can be scheduled.

On his way to becoming the National League Rookie of the Year, still the oldest player to be so honored, the thirty-three-year-old Jethroe had 1 hit in the Braves' 8–5 loss to the Cardinals before 3,517 in that historic, yet largely overlooked, game. Nicknamed "The Jet," Jethroe had a heralded career in the Negro Leagues and in the Cuban Winter Leagues before signing with Branch Rickey's Brooklyn Dodgers during the 1948 season. Three years before, according to a 1997 story in the *Atlanta Journal Constitution* by Jim Auchmutey, Rickey began interviewing Black players, including Jethroe, who acknowledged that he smoked and drank, and Rickey felt he needed to go with a more clean-cut pioneer. He selected Robinson. "He had everything Mr. Rickey wanted," Jethroe said of Robinson. "He was a college man who had experienced the white world, and I wasn't." With eventual Hall of Famer Duke Snider playing center field for the Dodgers, Rickey sold Jethroe's contract to the Braves after the 1949 season. It was later reported that Rickey regretted the move. The *New York Daily Mirror's*

Jackie Robinson (*left*) made his St. Petersburg debut in 1952 after Sam Jethroe (*right*) broke the city's color barrier with the Boston Braves in 1950. *Courtesy of the Boston Public Library, Leslie Jones Collection.*

Gus Steiger quoted him as saying, "It might be the biggest mistake I ever made in baseball." Jethroe played three years in the majors with the Braves, leading the National League in stolen bases twice.

On March 1, 1951, as part of a plan to swap training sites with the Yankees for one year, the New York Giants opened their temporary camp at Miller Huggins Field, bringing about an important first. Future Hall of Fame outfielder Monte Irvin, third baseman Hank Thompson, catcher Ray Noble and shortstop Artie Wilson were in the Giants' camp—the first Black players to train in the city. According to E.H. McLin of the *St. Petersburg Times*, the four players lodged at a private home on Fifth Avenue South.

"We couldn't stay with the team," Irvin recalled years later to Bill Francis of the National Baseball Hall of Fame and Museum. "So I went to Eddie Brannick, our traveling secretary, one day and I said, 'You know, Eddie, we're here trying to make the team and look like we're going to become a vital part of this team. Why are we treated so badly?' He said,

'Monte, it's the state law. Everything is segregated, including the hotels, the restaurants, the theaters and the buses. That's the way it is and that's the way it's going to be until somebody changes it. They haven't changed it yet. We hope they do.'"

For the first time, Al Lang Field offered a special section in the grandstand for people of color, due to the efforts of Al Lang and the city's recreation director, Pierce Gahan. The section remained open during the Florida International League season and would remain until Al Lang Field was desegregated in 1962.

On March 10, Irvin, Wilson and Thompson were all in the lineup, and Noble entered the game midway as the Giants dropped their home debut, losing to the Cardinals, 4–2, in front of 6,654. Little was made of their presence.

Unlike those Black pioneers before him, Jackie Robinson never went unnoticed, certainly not on April 2, 1952, the day of his Al Lang debut. A Dodgers-Yankees matchup was always a big draw anywhere, but with Jackie, the crowds were record-breaking. Of the top eleven all-time best-attended Grapefruit League games in St. Petersburg, five were games with Jackie in the lineup. His seven games drew 52,032, an average of 7,433, and Jackie rarely disappointed. In those seven games, Robinson batted .346 with 3 doubles and a home run.

Stories began appearing in local newspapers touting number 42's arrival two days before. Extra temporary bleacher seats were built at Al Lang Field, a practice that would continue for all of Robinson's games there. Fans spent the night outside the park's box office in order to get tickets. The Jordan Park Community Club bought a block of three hundred tickets. Most Black-owned businesses closed at noon the day of the game in anticipation of the 2:00 p.m. start, and several large white firms made arrangements to allow minority employees to attend the game. Wrote the *Times*: "A committee of well-known Negroes at the request of Al Lang was named to the official welcoming committee. Negro fans came from as far north as Jacksonville and as far south as Fort Myers. Hundreds of others came from Tampa, Gainesville, Palatka, DeLand, Orlando, Punta Gorda and High Springs."

The welcoming committee greeted Jackie and two teammates, catcher Roy Campanella and pitcher Joe Black, in a pregame ceremony. Recognizing his contributions to the YMCA, Jackie was given a lifetime membership to the Melrose Park YMCA before the game and, among all of the hoopla, somehow found time to meet with youngsters from the Police Athletic League.

A St. Petersburg spring training record crowd of 8,809 attended the game at Al Lang Field on March 29, 1953. In what many believe was the greatest game ever played on the waterfront, the Dodgers edged the Yankees, 1–0, a preview of the upcoming World Series. Many were there to see Jackie Robinson, who scored the only run of the game. Tampa Bay Times *photo.*

E.H. McLin, of the *Times*' News of the Negro Community section, described the scene this way: "More than half of the attendance was colored. Every available space in the park was occupied. The section of the grandstand marked 'Colored' was filled long before game time and so was most of the West section of the grandstand from the top to the bottom."

Cal Adams's column in that same section of the newspaper was written with mixed emotions. "Throughout the game we watched the conduct and thought it to be the best we've seen," he wrote. "However, the dire need for Negroes dropping certain prejudices was most evident in the game. We have to learn that excelling in sports is not restricted to race or creed. Regardless of a person's color he should be given applause when merited."

This was prompted after Yankees rookie third baseman Andy Carey made what Yankee writers claimed was the team's best play of the spring on a foul pop hit by Jackie Robinson; accounts described the reaction among Black fans as muted.

That first game was only the beginning of his popularity on the waterfront. Those on hand that Wednesday afternoon were part of a city record crowd of 7,759 that saw the Dodgers thump the Yankees, 11–1. Robinson contributed 2 doubles, 1 walk, 2 runs batted in and participated in three double plays. Fellow future Hall of Famer Roy Campanella had two of the team's 9 doubles, most of which bounced into the temporary bleachers.

According to *St. Petersburg Times* sports editor Bill Beck, Robinson "had more than his share of fans. No matter what Jackie did—once it was reach up and grab a pop fly without moving out of his tracks—he drew a blast of cheering from the bleachers banked along the left field wall where Negro customers were solid. When Jackie lashed out his brace of doubles the din was terrific."

"It was gratifying to us to note how hard Baseball Ambassador Al Lang worked to make the Negro fans comfortable at the park," wrote the *Times'* McLin.

In fact, the entire park personnel did the very same thing. After several innings we observed hundreds of fans milling around the front entrance trying to purchase tickets but they were all gone even all standing room. The crowd was orderly, conducted themselves with decorum.

There was a sign and a rope which designated the "colored section" at the lower end of the first base line. Al Lang had field attendants remove the rope, but the sign remained. The removal of the rope was a sign of progress. However, we knew that more Negroes would occupy grandstand seats than the allotted space could and would, hold. We also knew once that section was filled to capacity. Negroes would begin to sit wherever possible. Before the game got underway, we had seen our prediction come true and seating had become democratic. This mannerly order by which seating was done was one of the best signs of progress we've seen in our travels. Negroes living in other cities, both north and south, would have been amazed to see how well the mixed audience enjoyed the game. In Atlanta, they would not believe such an incident was possible in the Deep South. For there they only know the park has a grandstand because they see it.

The following week, Reverend Ben Wyland, executive secretary of the United Churches of Greater St. Petersburg, extended an invitation to Black citizens to attend Easter Sunday services at Al Lang for the first time.

Of course, the news wasn't all good. Two weeks after Robinson's debut, under the headline "Dodgers Glad to Say Goodbye to Dixie" in *The Sporting*

News, there was this report: "Some of the Dodgers openly expressed their happiness in getting out of the Deep South this year, according to the experts traveling with the team. Jackie Robinson especially had a tough time."

As exciting as Jackie's St. Petersburg debut was, it was his third game there on March 29, 1953, that local and New York media unhesitatingly called the greatest game ever played in St. Petersburg. "It had," wrote the *Times*, "almost as much World Series atmosphere as the classic itself."

Brooklyn's 1–0 win drew what still remains the all-time city record: 8,809. Robinson walked, doubled and scored the only run of the game between two teams that had faced each other six months earlier in the World Series and would do so again in another six months. Robinson, who scored on Campanella's ground-ball out between third base and shortstop, was the only runner of the game to reach third. As he did in the 1952 World Series, Dodgers right fielder Carl Furillo made two defensive gems to keep the Yankees off the scoreboard. While Jonny Podres worked six innings to earn the win, Joe Black worked the final three frames and faced Casey Stengel's pinch-hitters, Mickey Mantle (HOF 1974), Yogi Berra (HOF 1972) and Johnny Mize (HOF 1981), in the ninth inning to complete the save. Black walked Mantle and retired Berra, but not before the Yankees catcher blasted one over the right-field fence, foul by five feet. Mize was the final out, fouling out to third baseman Bobby Morgan, the only Dodger on the left side of the infield due to the infield shift.

Louis Effrat of the *New York Times* wrote: "Remove the palm trees, take the beautiful bay from the background, change the date, reduce the temperature by thirty degrees and Al Lang Field might have been Ebbets Field or Yankee Stadium today. Certainly, it was a World Series setting."

St. Petersburg Times columnist Jack Elllison shared: "Enterprising fans parked two open trucks on Bay Shore Drive alongside the third base side of the park and crammed several dozen neighbors into the truck bodies to view the game for free. Even more enterprising spectators climbed the fence and hopped down into the park, but no one seemed to mind." The Dodgers were back at Al Lang two days later. The game, won by the Yankees, 4–2, on the strength of a Berra home run, drew 6,751, bringing the total attendance for the two-game set with the Dodgers to 15,559. As a result, attendance for the 1953 season at Al Lang for twenty-five dates was a record 85,970.

Robinson's final game at Al Lang Field was another re-creation of the previous World Series and was played on March 29, 1956, before 8,468 fans, the second-largest crowd in St. Petersburg's spring training history. Soot Zimmer, whose husband, Don, played shortstop for the Dodgers that day, attended the game with her father. "The crowd was so big we sat in a temporary section in the outfield, but we did have seats," Soot told me. "Everywhere you looked there were people." The Dodgers won, 5–4, in ten innings when newly acquired third baseman Randy Jackson's bloop double was mishandled by Yankee right fielder Joe Collins, allowing Gino Cimoli to score from first. The Dodgers scored 4 runs in the first off Yankees ace Whitey Ford (HOF 1974), an outburst that included a home run by Robinson.

It was a magical day, especially for seven-year-old Steve Garvey, the Dodgers' batboy that day. Just twenty-four hours earlier, Steve was like so many other local seven-year-olds: getting ready for Tampa's Little League baseball season and counting down the days until he would no longer be a second grader.

"My dad is a Greyhound bus driver and a big Dodgers fan," Garvey began recounting the day to me.

> *He comes home one evening in late March, months after the Dodgers had finally beaten the Yankees in the World Series, and when we sit down, he asks me if I want to skip school the next day. I said, "Well yeah, where are we going?" He said, "I have a charter to pick up the Brooklyn Dodgers from the Tampa Airport to take them to St. Pete to play the Yankees in an exhibition game, and I think it might be a good day for you and me."*

He wasn't wrong. The next day was a Thursday, and at 8:00 a.m., with his Topps baseball cards in hand, Steve stood on the tarmac outside the bus as the Dodgers' DC-7 team plane—the *Kay O'Malley 1*, named after the wife of the Dodgers' owner, Walter O'Malley—taxied down the runway before coming to a stop. The players deplaned and filed past the nervous youngster. "It was like they were walking right off their baseball cards," Steve recalled. "Finally, the last two guys come strolling along and it was [Roy] Campanella and Jackie [Robinson], and all of a sudden they stopped. Jackie looks at me and looks at my dad, who is wearing his gray uniform with his name tag, and Jackie says 'Joe, does your son play baseball?' And my dad tells him that we are going to be starting up the season the following Saturday."

"Well, kid," Garvey remembered Robinson responding, "if you practice hard and work hard, maybe you will be a Dodger someday." There may never have been a more prophetic statement.

The best day of Garvey's young life was about to get even better. When Joe pulled the Dodgers' team bus into the parking lot at Al Lang twenty minutes later, a short, stout man with boxer shorts and a strap T-shirt greeted them and asked Steve if he wanted to be the team's batboy that day.

A few seconds later, he was whisked away and assigned to taking the Dodgers' bats and helmets out to the field with assistance from Joe. It wasn't long before he found himself playing catch with first baseman Gil Hodges.

At the same time a few feet away, Yankees center fielder Mickey Mantle, who would hit a major-league-high 52 home runs that year, began his round of batting practice. As excited as he was about playing catch with his dad's favorite player, Steve became distracted as Mantle bashed ball after ball over the left-field fence and into the waters of Tampa Bay. Not surprisingly, one of Hodges's throws hit him right in the chest.

Seven-year-old Tampa native Steve Garvey served as the Dodgers' batboy for Jackie Robinson's last game in St. Petersburg in 1956. Gil Hodges was among the eight future Hall of Famers who played on that Dodgers team. *Courtesy of Steve Garvey.*

"Hodges came over to see if I was all right, and then he asked me, 'You weren't watching Mickey hit, were you?' I said, 'Yes, sir.' He said, 'Son, we're the world champions.' After that, I didn't watch Mickey hit anymore. I think it was my first teachable moment outside the family."

At one point during the game, while Steve was on the bench conversing with Hodges and shortstop Pee Wee Reese, Robinson, not seeing the youngster, almost sat on top of him. "He immediately apologized, and I said, 'That's OK. Show and Tell is Monday, and boy, am I going to have a great time.'"

For the next six years, as his father drove the team buses out of Tampa, the younger Garvey was able to serve as a batboy for various Grapefruit League games in the Tampa Bay area, including those of the Yankees, Tigers and Cardinals.

Twelve years later, as Robinson had forecast, the Dodgers selected Garvey out of Michigan State with the first selection in the secondary phase of the June draft. He played first base for the Dodgers for thirteen years, and his 1,727 games played are third all time. And, in the spring of 1979, like Robinson, he, too, would hit a home run out of Al Lang.

But on that one day in March 1956, Garvey was living a dream. "It wasn't just my baptism into baseball," remembered Garvey. "It was such a great part of my growing up, and with players like Robinson, Campanella and Jim Gilliam; it was such an important era on baseball's timeline. To be around my idols and watch and listen to and talk with them was a great foundation for falling in love with the game. And lo and behold, twelve years after that first day of being the batboy, I was drafted in the first round by the Dodgers."

Al Lang Field hosted many other Black pioneers throughout the 1950s, including Larry Doby, Elston Howard, Tom Alston, George Crowe, Don Newcombe, Ed Charles and Hank and Tommy Aaron.

LARGEST SPRING TRAINING CROWDS, ST. PETERSBURG HISTORY

March 29, 1953	8,809	Yankees-Dodgers*
March 29, 1956	8,468	Yankees- Dodgers*
March 16, 1958	7,872	Yankees-Braves
April 2, 1952	7,759	Yankees-Dodgers*
March 12, 1977	7,729	Cardinals-Mets
March 12, 1947	7,706	Yankees-Cardinals
March 26, 1954	7,702	Yankees Dodgers*
March 11, 1950	7,701	Yankees-Cardinals
March 17, 1968	7,280	Cardinals–Red Sox
March 10, 1959	7,238	Yankees-Braves
March 25, 1955	7,212	Yankees-Dodgers*

*Jackie Robinson in lineup

• • • •

March 18, 1952
The Braves edged the Yankees, 1–0, in fourteen innings, as Warren Spahn faced Vic Raschi. Spahn worked six innings and Raschi five, so neither was around when Braves first baseman George Crowe lined a double off the left-field fence to score Billy Bruton with the only run of the game. Crowe was a pioneer for minorities in many ways; he helped break down barriers in two sports. The State of Indiana's first "Mr. Basketball," Crowe played ball at Indiana Central College and briefly with the Harlem Globetrotters. He also was a member of the first Black basketball team to play at Madison

Square Garden. As if that wasn't enough, Crowe was a veteran of World War II and played two seasons in the Negro Leagues before signing with the Braves in 1949 at the age of twenty-eight.

March 18, 1953
They started their game against the Yankees as the Boston Braves, but by the time their 5–3 setback ended, they had become the Milwaukee Braves by vote of the National League owners at the Vinoy Hotel, less than a mile from Al Lang Field. News of the transfer broke in the sixth inning of the game and overshadowed five innings of no-hit pitching by Braves rookie Bob Buhl. The change ended a seventy-seven-year relationship between the Braves and Boston.

March 10, 1954
Elston Howard, the first African American to wear the Yankees uniform, did so for the first time and slammed a triple, driving in 2 runs in a 4–3 win over the Washington Senators. Three days earlier, in the spring opener against the Yankees, the Cardinals dressed their first Black player, Tom Alston, a North Carolina A&T graduate who appeared as a pinch-hitter in the ninth inning of a 10–7 loss to the Yankees.

March 13, 1954
Newly acquired Braves outfielder Bobby Thomson, the New York Giants star of 1951, slid into second base at Al Lang Field and broke his ankle in the eighth inning of Milwaukee's 3–2 loss to the Yankees. The injury opened the door for a twenty-year-old rookie named Hank Aaron, who was in right field that day, his first game at Al Lang. Thomson didn't return until mid-July, and Aaron went on to finish fourth in the National League Rookie of the Year voting with a .280 batting average and 13 home runs.

March 23, 1954
Legendary actors Jimmy Stewart and June Allyson, director Tony Mann and a small crew were present at Al Lang during the Cardinals' pregame batting practice to film a scene for the movie *Strategic Air Command* (1955). Stewart was wearing a Cardinals uniform as the fictional third baseman Dutch Holland, who

Legendary actors Jimmy Stewart and June Allyson at Al Lang during the Cardinals' pregame batting practice on March 23, 1954, to film a scene for the movie *Strategic Air Command*, which was released in 1955. Strategic Air Command, *copyright Paramount Pictures.*

had just signed a contract with the Cards but is called to active duty. The scene in the movie lasts four minutes and needed to be completed before the start of the Cardinals-Braves game that day. The Cardinals beat the Braves, 6–5, behind six shutout innings from Vic Raschi.

March 26, 1955
The Yankees' sixty-five-year-old manager, Casey Stengel, was arrested by St. Petersburg police for assaulting a photographer from the *St. Petersburg Independent*, who charged that Stengel kicked him and cursed him in the first inning of the Yankees-Dodgers game two days earlier. According to Marty Appel's book *Casey Stengel: Baseball's Greatest Character*, Stengel called Yankees publicity director Bob Fishel to bail him out of the city jail. The next day, amid catcalls from the stands, an emotionless Stengel received the keys to the city from Mayor Samuel G. Johnson as part of a pregame ceremony honoring the thirtieth anniversary of the Yankees' arrival in St. Petersburg. Later that week, the photographer dropped the charges, Casey apologized and the two shook hands on the field, several feet away from where the alleged incident occurred.

January 14, 1956
If you were one of the three thousand fans who attended the First Old Timers game at Al Lang to benefit the March of Dimes, you saw Truett Banks "Rip" Sewell, known as the inventor of the eephus pitch, strike out Jimmie Foxx (HOF 1951), who swung and

missed at three of Sewell's famous blooper pitches that reached an arc of twenty-five feet. Never mind they were both forty-nine years of age at the time. The game was played annually at Al Lang Field until it was switched to Clearwater's Bright House Network Field in 2004.

March 10, 1956

Yankees centerfielder Mickey Mantle threw out the Cardinals' Wally Moon at the plate with two outs in the bottom of the ninth to keep their game scoreless. Moon was trying to score on Pete Whisenant's bouncing single to center. Two innings later, the same scenario developed again, only this time, Mantle's throw was a bit wide, Moon scored and the Cards won, 1–0, on Whisenant's walk-off single. A sunny Sunday afternoon crowd of 7,200 looked on.

March 11–12, 1956

Mickey Mantle, the 1956 Triple Crown winner, kicked off his best spring. The switch-hitting centerfielder led the Yankees to wins over the Cardinals and White Sox with mammoth home runs on back-to-back days. Against the Cardinals, his eighth-inning, opposite-field, 3-run homer to left off Bob Mabe bounced into Tampa Bay on one hop and provided a 4–3 win. The next day, he did it again, sending a home run into the bay to help make a 4–2 winner out of Whitey Ford over the Sox's seven-time All-Star Billy Pierce. He finished the spring with 5 homers in St. Pete, his best total ever.

March 17, 1956

Mickey Mantle's 420-foot, walk-off, 2-run home run in the ninth gave the Yankees a 7–5 win over Detroit on St. Patrick's Day. The Mick had a homer, a triple and 2 singles and made a great catch in center field to rob first baseman Earl Torgeson of an extra-base hit.

March 14, 1957

The league enacted an experimental twenty-second rule for pitchers for the A's-Cardinals game. Plate umpire Hal Dixon called a violation on the Cards' Herm Wehmeier, and on the very next pitch, Kansas City's Gus Zerniel homered, a ball that bounced into Tampa Bay as the A's won, 5-4. Alvin Dark and Hal Smith also homered for the A's.

April 3, 1957
In an 8–5, ten-inning loss to the Tigers, Stan Musial hit a third-inning, game-tying home run off Tigers ace Frank Lary. The drive smashed the bulbs on a light pole 60 feet above the 385-foot marker in right-centerfield. Tigers first baseman Earle Torgeson delivered a 3-run triple to right center in the top of the tenth to provide the winning margin.

April 4, 1957
Perhaps the best pitching duel in waterfront history unfolded as Hall of Famers Whitey Ford and Robin Roberts faced off. Ford's Yankees won it, 1–0, over the Phillies in ten innings. Roberts went eight innings, allowing only 1 hit; Ford went seven innings, permitting only 5. New York right fielder Woodie Held delivered a triple in the tenth, only the Yankees' second hit of the game, and he scored on shortstop Gil McDougald's walk-off sacrifice fly.

12

YEAR-ROUND BALL

As major league teams began gathering for spring training in 1948, the Associated Press noted that 45 percent of the players who were about to report were rookies, believed to be a record. While the youthful St. Louis Browns had something to do with that, this development signaled a new trend, a different direction for a growing number of clubs: to hasten the development of their top prospects. Not long after, new Yankees manager Casey Stengel opened the first pre–spring training rookie camp in St. Pete, and Branch Rickey opened his spring training workouts to Dodgers rookies and veterans alike at Vero Beach. Other clubs followed with separate camps for their prized youngsters.

The Cardinals, too, were one of those teams with a separate rookie camp, but by the mid-1950s the team's creative general manager, Frank Lane, began laying the blueprint for what he saw as the next logical step, an off-season league for prospects. It took convincing some of his peers, but in two years' time, the Florida Winter Instructional was in place. While a bit different, it is still in practice today.

On September 19, 1958, the four-team, 48-game league was formally announced, with play to begin in less than a month. Al Lang Field was, of course, one of the parks where the new innovation debuted. The Cardinals and Yankees shared Al Lang, the Milwaukee Braves were at Braves Field in Bradenton and the Kansas City Athletics were at Al Lopez Field and Plant Field in Tampa. Originally, none of the players chosen for the squads could have more than three years of professional experience. The Yankees won the inaugural FIL game over the Braves, 4–3, at Al Lang on October 15 in front of 3,893, all guests of the local merchants who purchased the tickets. Among the prospects in the game were Bob Uecker, Tommy Aaron (younger brother of Hank) and future Yankees Joe Pepitone and Phil Linz. Later that season, on December 6, seventeen-year-old Ray Sadecki, who was pitching in the major leagues nineteen years later, threw a no-hitter against the Yankees' instructional league team, striking out 12 and walking 7. His pitch count was not made available. The instructional league, which helped propel the career of hundreds of major league players, was held at Al Lang through the fall of 1987.

And while it was ostensibly designed to be just as the name implies, Tommy Zimmer, son of Don Zimmer, had his own different view of Al Lang's instructional league games. Zimmer, who played with the FIL Cardinals in the early seventies, told me, "We played to win, and sometimes the other team didn't like it. Most times, you were there to learn, to work on something, but playing for [Cardinals legendary instructor] George Kissell, you were also there to learn how to win. A lot of the guys weren't big on playing instructional league, but for me, it was in my hometown, and it was a job. I used to ask George if he needed any catchers."

While most of the players in the instructional league were younger prospects, Zimmer pointed out that this father, Don, went to the instructional league with the Senators in 1964 at age thirty-three to become a catcher at the request of his manager, Gil Hodges.

Bill Ripken, who went to instructional league at Al Lang with the Orioles, had this memory of facing the Cardinals and the Mets. "It was a pretty cool stadium, as opposed to playing on open fields like many of them were in the instructional league. Then seeing how advanced some of the players were, like Vince Coleman and Terry Pendleton for the Cardinals, it was just a different level. The Mets had Doc Gooden, Floyd Youmans, Rick Aguilera and Randy Myers, that was a major league staff. It was like a whole different dynamic playing there."

So close to the big leagues but yet sometimes so far. "We played a game there, and during the entire game, they were pressure-washing the seats," remembered Ripken. "A 10:00 a.m. game with four pressure washers going at the same time. Couldn't hear a thing and left the park with a huge headache. Very far from the big leagues."

Another former Oriole, Hall of Famer Jim Palmer, pitched in the instructional league in 1968, when he was essentially told his career was over. The twenty-three-year-old Palmer had pitched sparingly the previous two seasons due to a torn rotator cuff. At a game at Al Lang, he surrendered 8 runs and 12 hits in a loss to the Twins. "Earl Weaver said he wouldn't give a nickel for Jim Palmer pitching in the big leagues again," Palmer told me. "I also remember how pretty the bay looked out there in left field and I remember a few of the home runs I gave up that day were headed toward the bay."

But the eventual three-time Cy Young Award winner got the last laugh. Palmer switched his anti-inflammatory at the suggestion of a trainer from the National Basketball Association's Baltimore Bullets, his arm recovered and, that following season, Weaver's first full year as manager of the Orioles, Palmer went 16-4 and posted a 2.34 ERA, second best in the American League. The team won 109 games and the 1969 AL pennant. The following winter, another future Hall of Famer, Bert Blyleven, pitched in the instructional league and then helped lead the Twins to the AL West title. Mark "The Bird" Fydrich pitched in the instructional league in 1975 and was American League Rookie of the Year in 1976. The Tigers' sensational double-play combination of Lou Whitaker and Alan Trammell played together there in 1977, as did Pete Rose, Gary Carter, Steve Carlton, Joe Torre and many other major leaguers.

• • • •

February 27, 1958
After the Cardinals worked out and held photo day for the media in the morning, the Harlem Globetrotters defeated the Honolulu Surf Riders, 46–43, that evening. The speed of play was hampered significantly thanks to a pregame shower that soaked the court, located in Al Lang's infield. A crowd of 2,700 was on hand.

March 16, 1958
Before a Sunday crowd of 7,872, the third largest ever on the waterfront, the two reigning league champions faced off. The Yankees beat their World Series tormentors, the Braves, 4–1. It was the first major league game to be televised from St. Petersburg and was carried by WPIX back to New York, but not shown locally. WPIX utilized three cameras from points behind third base, first base and home plate. Mel Allen, Red Barber and Phil Rizzuto handled the commentary.

August 22, 1958

The St. Pete Saints became the first Florida State League team to win 100 games when they beat the Cocoa (Indians), 3–0, in the first game of a doubleheader before 5,362 fans at Al Lang. For winning both halves of the FSL seasons, players received a bonus of $43.75.

December 20, 1958

Al Lang hosted football for the first time as part of a four-year deal to host the National Association of Intercollegiate Athletics (NAIA) championship game, known as the Holiday Bowl. The games were held at Al Lang in 1958 and 1959 and at Stewart Field at St. Petersburg High School in 1957 and 1960. In the first game at Al Lang, Northeast Oklahoma State (Redmen) defeated the Arizona State College Lumberjacks, 19–13. Attendance was 8,628, and an estimated 15 million people watched via CBS-TV. In the 1959 game, the Texas A&I defeated the Lenior Rhyne

Al Lang was the site of the college football Holiday Bowl in 1958 and 1959. *Courtesy of the St. Petersburg Museum of History.*

Bears, 20–7, before 9,500 fans and a national TV audience. That crowd remains the largest to see a sporting event at Al Lang. On March 16, 1961, the NAIA announced it was moving the game to Sacramento, California, for two reasons: lack of a commitment from the city to build a football stadium as originally promised, and the city's segregationist tendencies. In the final game in St. Petersburg, one of the participating teams, Humboldt State of California, was forced to house its Black players separately. Thirty years earlier, one man had urged the city to follow Miami's lead (it built the Orange Bowl in 1937), but the plans never developed. That man? Al Lang. The city tried to revive the partnership with the NAIA in 1964, but efforts failed.

March 22, 1959
Cardinals nonroster rookie pitcher Bob Gibson—on the AAA Rochester roster—pitched six innings and held the impending World Series champion Dodgers to 1 run and 5 hits in his first win in a major league uniform as the Cards prevailed, 3–1, despite getting only 3 hits. St. Louis scored runs on a wild pitch, a throwing error and a fielding error.

March 28, 1959
In the afternoon, recently acquired Cardinals outfielder Bill White homered in his Al Lang debut before 3,136 spectators. In the evening, presidential hopeful John F. Kennedy made his debut at Al Lang, urging a crowd of about 1,000 to utilize the talents of its senior citizens. Both would become president: Kennedy of the United States in 1961 and White of the National League in 1989.

13

UNDER ONE ROOF

The 1960s brought about a multitude of societal changes that did not bypass baseball or Al Lang Field. We saw civil rights activists make their voices heard throughout Florida spring training cities. We were introduced to culture change as, thankfully, more minorities made major league rosters. We stretched boundaries, as new major league franchises sprang up in New York, Washington, Minneapolis, Houston and Los Angeles. We lost leaders. The press box even had a radical look. In his book *Vintage St. Pete*, Bill DeYoung noted that actress Marilyn Monroe "watched spring training games from the press box at Al Lang" with her ex-husband, Joe DiMaggio, who served as a Yankees "guest" coach for two weeks in 1961.

The decade began with the worst news: Al Lang died. At age eighty-nine, the greatest baseball ambassador any city ever had succumbed to pneumonia at St. Petersburg's St Anthony's Hospital in the early morning of February 27, 1960, the day after the Cardinals' first workout of the spring at the park bearing his name. "In a way," said Cardinals general manager Bing Devine, "he waited to see that we were all here and happy one more year. And then, this morning, he died." His Yankees' counterpart, George Weiss, said, "Modern day St. Petersburg is his monument."

Twenty-five years before, sportswriter Fred Lieb had this exchange with Commissioner Kenesaw Mountain Landis: "'Doesn't this fellow [Lang] ever get tired of boosting his hometown?' Landis asked me. 'I'm afraid not,' was my reply. 'He'll be talking of St. Petersburg's sunshine as he enters the Pearly Gates.'" No doubt he was.

While his longtime dream of bringing all sixteen major league teams to Florida to train would not be attained (it was twelve at the time of his death), Lang's efforts shone like the Florida sunshine he cherished. Less than three months after his death, E.C. Robison, Lang's successor as chairman of the city's baseball committee, reported to the St. Petersburg Chamber of Commerce that the city reaped the benefit of 1,145,000 words filed by sportswriters during the 1960 major league baseball spring training season, according to Western Union. Also included were 3,922 hours of time on baseball radio networks. He also revealed that 71 percent of tourists polled that spring gave major league baseball as their main reason for visiting St. Pete.

Both the Yankees and Cardinals canceled their afternoon workouts to allow players to attend Lang's funeral on March 1. At the service, they were all there; one thousand mourners were inside Christ Methodist Church, including honorary pallbearers baseball commissioner Ford Frick, past American League president Will Harridge, American League president Joe Cronin, National League president Warren Giles and the esteemed Branch Rickey, as well as many past and current players, front office executives and newspapermen. Estimates put the number outside the church at two thousand.

Upon returning to the field, Stan Musial, when asked how he felt in his sixteenth spring in St. Pete, answered: "I don't feel much different than I did in 1942. The only difference is Al Lang should be walking around the field enjoying this great weather."

While spring training in St. Petersburg was a paradise for many players, media and fans, it was a much different experience for others. By the 1960s, there were nearly sixty Black major leaguers training in Florida. What they found, as Bill White wrote in his book *Uppity: My Untold Story About the Games People Play*, was that racism "in Florida was constant, inescapable and all-pervasive—and it was codified in the state law." And its roots were deep. On the same day as of one of the city's greatest baseball celebrations— February 23, 1925, when the New York Yankees held their first-ever workout at Crescent Lake Park in the morning—some 2,500 members of the Ku Klux Klan held a nighttime parade and rally at Waterfront Park, three days before the Braves would begin their spring workouts there. It was a front-page story in both St. Petersburg newspapers. The Yankees story was on page nine of the *St. Petersburg Times*.

Fourteen years after Jackie Robinson made his major league debut, baseball—like other sports—still presented an uneven playing field for

Blacks. Much of that inequity was found at Florida's spring training camps. In March 1961, three years before the Civil Rights Act, a "misunderstanding" involving player invitations to a St. Petersburg Chamber of Commerce breakfast sparked a successful civil rights protest that brought about the beginnings of much-needed change in spring training practices. Confusion as to who was invited and who wasn't created tension that burst into a national story when Black players on the Cardinals' roster—particularly Bill White—complained that they were not included. The Cardinals' director of public relations, Jim Toomey, maintained that race had nothing to do with who was invited. Rather, he said, given the early hour of the breakfast, the list of invitees he posted in the team's clubhouse at Al Lang Field targeted players whose spring residences were close to the St. Petersburg Yacht Club, site of the breakfast. That sentence, however was not included on the memo tacked to the clubhouse corkboard. According to Adam Henig in his book *Baseball Under Siege*, of the forty-eight players who attended the breakfast, only one person of color, Yankees catcher Elston Howard, attended. Unlike the Cardinals, the Yankees had invited their entire roster.

Unconvinced of Toomey's explanation, White sounded off to Joe Reichler of the Associated Press. "When will we be made to feel like humans?" White asked. "They invited all but the colored players. Even the kids who have never come to bat in a major league game were invited, that is, if they were White. I wanted very badly to go. I think I am a gentleman and can conduct myself properly. This thing keeps gnawing at my heart. I think about this every minute of the day."

It did not go unnoticed that White, a five-time All-Star first baseman who would go on to become the first African American play-by-play announcer in the major leagues and president of the National League, was upset. While officials from the city and both teams continued to maintain that race was not a factor in the invitations, this story and other earlier, unsourced stories written by Wendell Smith from Chicago's *Herald-American* newspaper helped bring a spotlight on the social injustices practiced by major league teams training in the South. The *St. Petersburg Times* described a gentlemen's agreement with the city that Black residents would build or live only in a certain area of the city.

Dr. Ralph Wimbish, a physician, director of the local chapter of the NAACP and a Gibbs High School graduate who grew up in St. Petersburg's Gas Plant District, was asked annually by the Cardinals and Yankees to help find housing for the African American players. He not only opened

Dr. Ralph Wimbish, a physician and director of the local chapter of the NAACP, was asked annually by the Cardinals and Yankees to help find housing for African American players. He stopped the practice to help bring about changes in 1961. *Courtesy of the Wimbish family.*

his own home but also urged others in the Black community to do so. Bob Gibson, Elston Howard, Curt Flood and Bill White, as well as visiting players, had all been guests at the Wimbish home, sometimes only to use the pool.

In 1961, however, Ralph and his wife, Bette, realized their generosity was actually contributing to the city's segregation. They would not be assisting the Yankees' three Black players or the Braves' five with housing that spring. Dr. Robert Swain, an oral surgeon who had built a six-unit apartment complex that he rented to Black Yankees and Cardinals players every spring, also took a stand, even though he would lose roughly $650 a week with the loss of the rentals.

The February 1 headline in the sports section of the *St. Petersburg Times* blared, "Wimbish Declines Usual Assistance, Negro Major Leaguers Face Housing Problems." In the story, Wimbish stated clearly, "I would like it understood that this is nothing personal. Elston Howard is a friend. But the time has come when more adequate provisions without discrimination should be provided by the clubs themselves."

Wimbish pointed out that in some cases, players were staying in one house but had to eat in another and those meals lacked the proper nutrition.

Almost a footnote, less than three weeks after the breakfast, the National Association of Intercollegiate Athletics (NAIA) announced it was pulling the Holiday Bowl college football game out of St. Petersburg. The city had hosted the game for the previous four years, two of those at Al Lang. One of the reasons for the NAIA's decision was segregated housing forced on Humboldt State, a participant in the 1960 game. It was a tumultuous time in the Sunshine City.

The day after Wimbish's announcement, Yankees co-owner Dan Topping issued this statement from New York: "Howard, Lopez and Gonder mean as much to our ballclub as any other ballplayers and we would very much like to have the whole team under one roof." The references were to the Black players on the team's roster, Elston Howard and Jesse Gonder, and Hector Torres, a native of Mexico.

Cardinals management passed it off as a local government issue. They would continue to stay at the Vinoy Hotel and the Yankees at the Soreno, both in the same hotel chain. The hotels were eager to retain their teams, as long as it was under the "same basis as we've always had them by making arrangements for some of the players outside," was how the Vinoy's Norvell Smith put it, according to the *St. Petersburg Times*.

Worse, Al Lang's successor, E.C. Robison, blamed the media.

It is most unfortunate that the integration issue has been raised and publicized so much by the press in relation to baseball. Baseball club owners naturally want harmony on their clubs and will make every effort, as they have in the past to see that the best possible living conditions are obtained for their players. They also are not happy that they are being put in the middle so to speak on an age old problem that more seriously affects certain areas of our country than others. The questions raised can have serious future complications. The Negro players on both the Yankees and Cardinals have been well taken care of in the past and will be equally well taken of this year and in the future.

Wrote the *St. Petersburg Times*: "Other front offices began to squirm under new and increased pressure but the general reaction was the same: Maybe they don't like the situation, but they're stuck with it. There's nothing they can do about it now. Next year, or the year after perhaps, but not now—the baseball clubs must abide by the traditions of the people whose land they have invaded for a couple of months each year." So, conditions changed very little that spring. "Much of this could have been avoided if [Dan] Topping had shown a little more determination in dealing with the synthetic Dixie Boy who manages the Soreno Hotel," wrote *New York Herald Tribune* columnist Stanley Woodward, who also called it a "poor fight" between the team and the hotel.

A few weeks later, on March 22, the reason for the Yankees' soft approach became known. Ending five months of speculation, Topping and the Yankees finally made it official that they would be moving to Fort Lauderdale for the 1962 Grapefruit League season, ending what had been the longest relationship between a major league team and a host city. Topping listed these factors in the Yankees' decision to move: a modern stadium with greater capacity than the six thousand seats at Al Lang; monopoly of local spring training baseball; exclusive possession for the training season of a motel in which Negro players would be welcome; and better all-around conditions insofar as ballclub welfare is concerned. Fort Lauderdale agreed to build a $600,000 stadium that would seat more than eight thousand, and their new spring hotel, the Oceanfront Yankee Clipper, welcomed all Yankees.

Simultaneously, the city announced that another New York team would be moving in. Technically, the Yankees' contract with St. Petersburg ran through 1962 unless a replacement tenant was found. Due to Major League Baseball's decision to add two expansion teams, there was one available. The first-year Mets agreed to move in with a five-year contract and a five-year option. Except for 1951, when the Yankees and Giants switched spring training sites, and during the three years (1943–45) when Florida spring training was prohibited due to wartime travel restrictions, the Yanks had called St. Petersburg home every March since 1925.

Two months after the disastrous chamber of commerce breakfast, another downtown St. Pete breakfast was held with members of the chamber and a group of business leaders known as the Committee of 100. It could have been themed "Do we want baseball?" as one attendee asked the large gathering according to the *St. Petersburg Times*. It was brought up at this meeting that for the previous three springs, the Cardinals had asked for upgrades to Al Lang, including an additional practice field, covered bullpens and upgrades to the clubhouse and press box. Recently, another request had been added to their list: the need for desegregated housing. With the Yankees gone, alarm bells were going off in the Suwannee Hotel ballroom that morning. Fortunately, the group was resolved. "What we really want to do is not just fix things up for the Cardinals," the committee's director, Walter Jerkins, told the *Times*. "We want to make sure everyone is agreed that St. Petersburg should be the best spring training base in baseball and is willing to do what is necessary to make it that way."

One thing was very clear: St. Petersburg and Florida were either going to change, or their economies were going to suffer. By the following spring, the physical improvements to Al Lang Field were complete. Slowly, begrudgingly, other changes began taking place. Around the state, major league teams began dropping the practice of staying at segregated hotels.

"Florida was really afraid of losing clubs to Arizona, that's what really pushed them," Bill White told me recently. "Arizona started trying to steal teams, and people don't realize it, but that helped about as much as anything else." And without Al Lang's presence—the master of it all—that fear became very real.

Backed by the support of the Major League Players Association, numerous teams, including the Cardinals and the incoming New York Mets, secured integrated housing. The Cardinals organization, according to Tim McCarver's book *Few and Chosen*, purchased the Outrigger Hotel just north of the Sunshine Skyway as their official headquarters, in part because of their fear that Blacks would boycott their Anheuser-Busch products. The Cards had some 130 members of their party staying at the Outrigger. The players themselves adapted much better than the city. "Hey," White told me, "we wanted to win."

In his book, White wrote, "For the first time, Black players felt comfortable bringing their families to spring training. Our kids went to integrated events organized by the players' wives. Black and White players and their families were even swimming in the same pool. All the integration was so unheard of in Florida that people would drive by the motel all day just to gawk and stare."

Bob Gibson credited team leaders for bringing the entire group together. "Several of the White players had traditionally stayed with their families in beachfront cottages during spring training, but when Musial and Boyer gave up their private accommodations to move in with the rest of the team—

Cardinals wives exercising together poolside at the Outrigger, the team hotel, just north of the Sunshine Skyway, in 1965. *Courtesy of St. Petersburg Museum of History.*

Segregation at Al Lang Field existed until 1962. *Courtesy of St. Petersburg Museum of History.*

Blacks included—the Cardinals had successfully broken down the local custom," he wrote in his book *Stranger to the Game*.

Cardinals Hall of Fame outfielder Lou Brock remembered sitting at the Outrigger talking baseball with Gibson, Boyer, Curt Flood and Curt Simmons, among others. "I probably learned more there than at any point in my life," Brock told the *St. Petersburg Times*. The Mets moved to the Colonial Inn on St. Petersburg Beach, where things were not quite the same. The affable veteran lefty pitcher Al Jackson became the first Black person to register at the hotel. Steve Jacobson, covering the Mets for *Newsday* at the time, described Jackson's first hours at the hotel this way in his book *Carrying Jackie's Torch*: "Jackson checked in and went to his room. The phone rang. The manager asked him to come to his office. He said the guests weren't used to seeing Blacks in the hotel; would Jackson do him a favor? Do not go into the bar, the restaurant and especially not the pool." Jacobson quoted Jackson as saying, "I thought, I'll be damned." As a result, the team created its own private dining room at the hotel and did not allow any players to enter the bar.

The Mets stayed at the Colonial Inn until moving to the new Hilton across the street from Al Lang in 1971. The Cardinals remained at the Outrigger (which became a Sheraton) until moving to the Travel Lodge in

Treasure Island in 1976. And in the spring of 1962, Al Lang Field and other parks, following the lead of Bill Veeck's Chicago White Sox at Payne Park in Sarasota, removed the "Colored Only" signs in an attempt to desegregate the grandstands. With the passing of the Civil Rights Act of 1964, all fifteen teams training in Florida were housing their players under one roof.

It was progress for the national pastime, but it would be another ten years before substantial civil rights advancements would be realized in St. Petersburg, and it would be an ugly sanitation workers' strike that brought to light the depth of the city's racial problems leading to that progress.

• • • •

March 23, 1960
Yankees rookies Johnny James and Bill Bethel combined to no-hit the Phillies, 4–0, on a sunny Wednesday afternoon. The Phils' only base runner was Johnny Callison, who drew a walk off James in the first inning. It was the Yankees' first ever no-hitter in exhibition play. Bethel would never reach the big leagues, and James won a total of 5 games in three years with the Yankees and Dodgers. Hall of Famer Robin Roberts, who brought 221 career wins into the matchup, was the loser.

March 25, 1960
Stan Musial's 3-run home run off the Reds' nineteen-game winner Cal McLish powered the Cardinals to an 8–3 win. The 410-foot blast to left-center was the 19th and last home run Musial would hit on the waterfront. It was eighteen years and six days since the first one.

March 29, 1960
Don Drysdale (HOF 1984) allowed 2 hits in seven innings to beat the Cardinals, 5–0. Seven days before, teammate Sandy Koufax (HOF 1972) beat the Yankees with six innings of 1-hit ball. Drysdale struck out 8 and walked none.

March 16, 1961
Six-time National League stolen-base champ Maury Wills stole a base, Duke Snider (HOF 1980) hit a home run and the Dodgers beat the Yankees, 6–1. Snider remains the franchise's all-time

home run leader to this day with 389 and has held that distinction since passing teammate Gil Hodges in 1956.

March 23, 1961
Mickey Mantle hit the last home run he would hit on the waterfront in a 4–3 loss to the Orioles, who swept the three-game season series from the Yankees. O's right fielder Whitey Herzog threw out the tying run at the plate in the eighth inning.

March 31, 1961
In a rematch of Game 7 of the previous Fall Classic, the Pirates again prevailed over the Yankees. Bill Mazeroski's walk-off home run gave Pittsburgh the series title six months before. On this day, Mazeroski was again the hero with a single, double and 3 RBIs in the Pirates' 4–1 win. And just like in Game 7, Harvey Haddix got the win and Ralph Terry the loss. It happened in front of 6,247 fans.

April 2, 1961
On a beautiful Easter Sunday, Yankees great Whitey Ford tossed a 6-hit, 1–0 win over the Reds in a preview of that season's World Series. Moose Skowron's homer in the second inning won it in front of a New York TV audience on WPIX.

April 5, 1961
After thirty-three years of training in St. Petersburg, the Yankees played their final game as the home team at Al Lang, recording an

Cardinals ace Bob Gibson (*left*), the winningest pitcher of all time on the waterfront, and teammate Ken Boyer helped with desegregating baseball's housing in Florida spring training cities. Tampa Bay Times *photo*.

eleven-inning, 5–4 walk-off win over the Cardinals. Roger Maris's single drove in the winning run as the Yankees won for only the third time in 15 games at the waterfront, their poorest spring ever. They would win 109 regular-season games and go on to win the World Series over the Reds. Sportswriter and historian Fred Lieb, who covered the Yankees' first game at Waterfront Park in 1925, threw out the ceremonial first pitch and wrote the game story for the *St. Petersburg Times*.

14

MEET THE METS

One month shy of thirty-eight years since he first wore a uniform on the waterfront and nearly two years since his last appearance there as manager of the Yankees, Casey Stengel returned to Al Lang Field to lead the 1962 Mets, one of two first-year National League expansion teams. And while the seventy-one-year-old future Hall of Famer with nine World Series rings (including seven as a manager) would soon begin his twenty-second year as a major league manager, his first official act of business in St. Petersburg was an entirely new role. Casey Stengel: author.

It didn't go well. Following the release of his new book *Casey at the Bat*, the Mets' new skipper was scheduled to fly in to Tampa from Los Angeles on a Friday evening in mid-February for two book signings and a press luncheon the next day at Maas Brothers Store in St. Pete. But stormy weather in the area forced the plane to go on to Miami, where he caught a scheduled nonstop flight to New York that made a special stop for him in Orlando. From there he bused to St. Petersburg, arriving at 4:30 a.m. at the Colonial Inn, where a sign greeted him: "Stengelese spoken here." Nevertheless, Stengel was at Maas Brothers the next morning at 10:30 greeting those in line. As he got up to speak at one of the signings, the microphone assaulted the group's ears with awful-sounding feedback. Stengel quipped, "Already they're heckling me and I haven't even taken the field," the *St. Petersburg Times* quoted him as saying.

As impressive as it was that he answered the bell for the book signing, it wasn't always that way. Don Zimmer, in his book *A Baseball Life*, wrote that when the Mets played at Al Lang, the players would watch as Stengel arrived, and they knew by his slumped shoulders if he had been out entertaining the writers until the late hours of the morning.

> *Casey would sit on the grass at the far end of the dugout, leaning up against a wire fence. I got off to a great start that spring hitting home runs all over the place, and Casey would give me a wink as if to say "nice going kid." During the course of those games, as he'd sit on the grass, his head would start to nod and as I watched him, I got to know that when he nodded for the third time he was off to sleep. Well, I couldn't resist needling him and when it happened, I'd run down to the end of the dugout and shout something like "Let's go now! Shake 'em up out there!" Casey would jolt up from his nap and give that wink.*

Casey's Opening Day lineup against the Cardinals at Al Lang was more suitable for an old-timers exhibition game. Not including twenty-five-year-old starting pitcher Jay Hook, the average age of the other eight starters was thirty-three. "Casey didn't know any of our names," wrote Zimmer. "You have to remember he was used to the Yankees where the same players—Mantle, Berra, Ford, Bauer, McDougald, Collins, Coleman and the others—were there year after year. This was an entire team of new faces for Casey and he'd simply call us different names every day and usually we knew who he meant."

A sellout crowd of 6,872 was on hand for the opener on Saturday, March 10. Robert Lypsyte of the *New York Times* began his game story this way: "Seven white yawls rocked idly and ineffectually at anchor in Tampa Bay today, in perfect harmony with the New York Mets at bat, in the field and on the mound. The boats moored behind the left-field fence of Al Lang Field here, at least went nowhere with grace. The Mets, playing their first major league exhibition game, lost to the St. Louis Cardinals, 8–0, without a trace of elan." The Mets managed only four hits, including a triple by Zimmer. Stan Musial threw out Richie Ashburn (HOF 1955) at the plate from left field in the third inning, the closest the Mets came to scoring their first run. The next day, they recorded their first win, 4–3, over the Cards in walk-off fashion when Elio Chacon's single scored Ashburn with two outs in the ninth. Among the many firsts: National Baseball Hall of Fame historian Lee Allen was trapped for more than an hour in a new bathroom located on the grandstand roof adjacent to the press box.

The Mets' debut may have been overshadowed by another. Beer was served at a St. Petersburg ballfield for the first time ever. Budweiser and

Left: Mets manager Casey Stengel and team owner Joan Payson prior to a game at Al Lang. Payson was the third woman ever to own a major league team. *Courtesy of St. Petersburg Museum of History.*

Below: A Mets-Cardinals sold-out game in 1966. New York's Jim Hickman takes the throw at first base. *Courtesy of St. Petersburg Museum of History.*

Busch Bavarian—both brewed by the family that owned the Cardinals—were served by the bottle.

The Mets' spring gave no indication they were about to lose a major league record 120 games that summer by holding their own in the Grapefruit League and winning a respectable 12 out of 27, only 28 fewer games than they would win over the next six months.

• • • •

March 16, 1962
Hank Aaron hit a 420-foot home run in the Braves' 8–6 loss to the Cardinals. Stan Musial had two RBI singles to lead the Cards. Aaron started at third base, something he did only 5 times in the 3,298 regular-season games of his career. Aaron was forced to start there when Braves manager Birdie Tebbetts listed Eddie Mathews (HOF 1978) at third, forgetting that Mathews didn't make the trip to St. Petersburg from the Braves' camp in Bradenton. Aaron was charged with one error, which led to an unearned run charged to Braves starter and loser Warren Spahn (HOF 1973).

March 22, 1962
The Yankees and Mets squared off for the first time, and, in the highlight of the spring, the Mets prevailed in walk-off fashion, 4–3, before 6,277 pro-Mets fans. The Mets' Joe Christopher led off the bottom of the ninth with a triple, and one out later, pinch-hitter Richie Ashburn singled to right center to end the game after the Yankees tied it with a run in the top of the frame.

March 28, 1962
The first-year Mets rallied for 3 runs with two outs in the ninth off future three-time Cy Young Award winner Sandy Koufax (HOF 1972) for a 4–3 win. A check-swing double by pinch-hitter Rod Kanehl scored 2 runs, tying the game, and Felix Mantilla singled home Kanehl.

July 26, 1962
Ferguson Jenkins made his Al Lang debut for the Miami Marlins a memorable one, as he pitched a seven-inning, complete-game two-hitter against the St. Pete Cardinals, winning, 4–0, in Florida State

League play. The nineteen-year-old Jenkins struck out 7 and walked 3 and helped the Marlins, a Phillies affiliate, earn a doubleheader split. Jenkins would return to Al Lang in the National League and again in the Senior Professional Baseball Association (SPBA). Fergie's last appearance at Al Lang came twenty-seven years later as a member of the SPBA. Pitching for the Winter Haven Super Sox, on November 6, 1989, Fergie pitched five innings against the St. Pete Pelicans and was in line for the win before the bullpen collapsed as the Sox fell, 10–9.

April 4, 1963

Stan Musial's last game on the waterfront was a 12–3 Cardinals win over the Twins. Stan went 1-for-3 with an RBI single. He would announce his retirement on August 12 of that season. In his nineteen seasons of training on the waterfront, Stan played in well over two hundred Grapefruit League games, more than any other player.

March 22, 1965

Little-known Mets right-hander Gary Kroll and southpaw Gordie Richardson combined to throw a no-hitter over the Pirates, winning, 6–0. It would be the only no-hitter the Mets would throw—spring training or otherwise—in their first forty-seven years. Only four Pirates reached base, three via walks by Kroll in the first inning. Richardson struck out Willie Stargell (HOF 1988) to end the game.

June 14, 1966

In the same season that his team won twenty-two straight games, his first as manager of the Florida State League's St. Petersburg Cardinals, Sparky Anderson's team played the longest game in baseball's first one hundred years: a twenty-nine-inning, six-hour and fifty-nine-minute marathon won by the Miami Marlins, 4–3, on June 14 at Al Lang. It began at 7:30 p.m. on June 14 and ended at 2:29 the following morning. Several days later, umpire Lou Benitiz, who arbitrated the marathon, said he didn't realize that there is a little-known league rule that makes it illegal for an inning to start after 12:50 a.m.

March 15, 1967
The Reds' Pete Rose, nursing a groin injury, made his spring debut. He went 0-for-2 in a "B" game against the Mets at the Huggins-Stengel complex, then hustled over to Al Lang, where he went 3-for-5 for the varsity with a 2-run homer run as a lefty and a 3-run homer hitting right-handed in an 11–6 Reds win.

March 17, 1967
The Red Sox beat the Mets, 23–18, the highest-scoring game in waterfront history. Trailing by 5 runs in the ninth, the Sox scored 10 in the ninth as fourteen men came to the plate. The Red Sox got 23 hits and 13 walks. It was an odd game, whereby both teams came to bat in the ninth trailing by 5 runs. Winds of thirty to forty miles per hour blew throughout the game. The St. Petersburg Yacht Club, directly across the street from the ballpark, flew gale-warning flags all afternoon, according to Jack Lang of *The Sporting News*.

March 25, 1967
Twenty-two-year-old Tom Seaver won his first game in a Mets uniform, allowing 3 hits and 1 run in five innings in an 8–1 win over Kansas City at Al Lang Field before 1,748 fans. He went on to win the NL Rookie of the Year and eventually three Cy Young Awards while training in St. Petersburg.

March 29, 1967
As a precursor to his Triple Crown season of 1967, Boston's Carl Yastrzemski hit 2 home runs and drove in 6 runs in a 10–9 win over the Cardinals, a preview of the World Series later that season. Cards third baseman Mike Shannon had 2 home runs and 2 singles.

15

THE DREAM SEASON

Of the more than 22,000 individuals who have played major league baseball, only 268 are in the Hall of Fame. That's a .011 percent chance of making it to Cooperstown. Former Hall of Fame president Jeff Idelson puts it this way: "It's akin to watching two baseball games that encompasses 100 players (25-man rosters) and determining the ONE player who is going to Cooperstown. That's how difficult it is to make the Hall of Fame." That's why Idelson described what happened at Al Lang in 1968 as "staggering."

The Mets and Cardinals combined to play twenty-seven games on the waterfront that spring. Those games included twenty-eight future Hall of Famers: Hank Aaron, Luis Aparicio, Johnny Bench, Lou Brock, Jim Bunning, Rod Carew, Steve Carlton, Orlando Cepeda, Roberto Clemente, Bob Gibson, Catfish Hunter, Reggie Jackson, Al Kaline, Harmon Killebrew, Tony LaRussa, Mickey Mantle, Eddie Mathews, Joe Morgan, Tony Oliva, Tony Perez, Brooks Robinson, Frank Robinson, Nolan Ryan, Tom Seaver, Willie Stargell, Joe Torre, Hoyt Wilhelm and Carl Yastrzemski.

ESPN's Tim Kurkjian said, "1968 was perhaps the apex of baseball's greatness and popularity. And no place personified baseball in 1968 like Al Lang Field." Kurkjian, the most recent winner of the Baseball Writers Association of America's Career Excellence Award, continued: "What happened there in that wonderful park is amazing, and it has to be some kind of a record."

Just how amazing? In Tropicana Field's twenty-four seasons, a total of twenty-six future Hall of Famers have played there. And as Idelson pointed out, in that group at Al Lang were "six players who would go on to join the exclusive 3,000-hit club and six others with more than 500 home runs, three 300-game winners, a guy with sixteen Gold Gloves at third base, a Triple Crown winner and a three-time MVP."

That spring we also saw a rematch of the previous World Series and two previews of the upcoming one. There was also Mickey Mantle's last appearance in St. Petersburg.

All over the course of twenty-eight days.

A Sunday afternoon St. Patrick's Day crowd of 7,280—Al Lang Field's largest crowd since 1958—saw the Red Sox score twice in the ninth off Steve Carlton to beat the Cardinals, 3–2, in a rematch of the 1967 World Series. Bob Gibson pitched the first five innings for St. Louis, retiring fourteen straight batters at one point. Sox right fielder Tony Conigliaro, who had been hit in the eye by a pitch from the Angels' Jack Hamilton on August 18, 1967, and missed the World Series, led off the ninth with a double. After an out, Reggie Smith followed with a triple off Carlton, and then Rico Petrocelli hit a sacrifice fly just deep enough in right for Smith to beat Bobby Tolan's throw. In the bottom of the ninth, Petrocelli speared Phil Gagliano's line drive at shortstop and turned it into a game-ending double play.

While the Tigers won the 1968 World Series from the Cardinals in seven games, St. Louis swept both games between the two at Al Lang that spring. On March 13, Bob Gibson beat Earl Wilson, 4–2. In the spring finale on the waterfront, the Cardinals edged the Tigers, 3–2, in walk-off style. With the scored tied in the bottom of the ninth, Gagliano tripled and Tolan singled him home. The two would meet again 179 days later on October 1 in the first game of the World Series. A third game was scheduled for St. Petersburg on April 8, but the game was canceled in observance of the National Day of Mourning for Dr. Martin Luther King.

And, on March 28, the Yankees beat the Mets, 5–1, in Mantle's last game at Al Lang. The Mick started at first base and recorded a single in two trips to the plate. Roy White pinch-ran for him after his third-inning single, and Andy Kosko replaced him at first. The crowd was 3,567. The following March 1 at a press conference at the Yankees' training camp in Fort Lauderdale, Mantle announced his retirement.

As if there wasn't enough news concerning the waterfront in 1968, on the next-to-last day of the calendar year, the Cardinals announced that the following spring Al Lang Stadium would become the first spring training

Bob Feller, Ozzie Smith, Bruce Sutter, Reggie Jackson, Hank Aaron and Rickey Henderson (*left to right*) wave to the crowd from the porch at the Hank Aaron Boyhood Home Museum in Mobile, Alabama. All of these men played at Al Lang. *Courtesy of Library of Congress.*

facility with Astroturf, which would cover the infield. It was essentially a test to see if they would opt for synthetic grass for Busch Stadium, which they did in 1970. Lang's turf remained until its successor, Al Lang Stadium, was erected in 1977.

• • • •

April 2, 1968
Twenty-two-year-old Cardinals rookie Bobby Tolan's straight steal of home in the eighth inning gave the Cards a 3–2 win over the Mets. Trying to break into the defending World Series champions' lineup, Tolan caught Mets reliever Don Shaw in a leisurely windup and slid in ahead of the tag by catcher J.C. Martin. Tolan's heroics spoiled the performance of rookie pitcher Nolan Ryan, who went five innings and allowed only 2 unearned runs while striking out 5.

April 4, 1968
The "Oakland" A's played their only game at Al Lang, and Hall of Famer Catfish Hunter worked six innings, allowing only 2 runs, to

earn a 12–2 win over St. Louis. Twenty-two-year-old right fielder Reggie Jackson, another star headed for Cooperstown, went 2-for-4 with 3 runs scored. The A's moved their spring training home from Bradenton to Mesa, Arizona, the following spring.

March 11, 1969

After an 0-3 start, the Miracle Mets earned their first win of the spring in front of only 458 fans on a cold, blustery day. It was the first of 121 wins for the 1969 world champions. The Mets handled the Phillies, 15–7, as Cleon Jones hit for the cycle. The paid attendance of 458 was labeled Al Lang's "all-time low as far as anyone can remember" by the *St. Petersburg Times*. Seven months and four days later, the Mets' season climaxed with an improbable 5–3 win over the Orioles in Game 5 of the World Series.

March 17, 1969

The Pirates-Cardinals game was rained out, breaking St. Petersburg's streak of 768 consecutive days of sunshine, a world record. Readers of the *Evening Independent* received a free edition of the paper that day, a promotion that had been started in 1910 by Lew Brown, the editor who said, "Customers would get a free edition of the paper if the sun didn't shine that day."

March 19, 1970

Cardinals ace Bob Gibson defeated Minnesota's Jim Perry, 3–1, with seven innings of 2-hit shutout ball. Both pitchers would win the Cy Young that year. Perry pitched five innings, allowing only 1 run.

March 28, 1971

Hall of Famer Joe Torre, who wore two different home uniforms at Al Lang as a player and manager, hit 3 home runs for the St. Louis Cardinals in a 13–2 win over the Twins. Torre hit 2 home runs off 229-game winner Luis Tiant and another off Jim Kaat, elected to the Hall of Fame in 2021. The 3 blasts give Torre 6 home runs at Al Lang that spring, the most since Joe DiMaggio hit a record 7 in 1946. The Cards' catcher went on to win National League Most Valuable Player laurels that season. Bob Gibson pitched five scoreless innings for the win.

March 13, 1973
In his first plate appearance ever at Al Lang, forty-two-year-old centerfielder Willie Mays (HOF 1979) slammed a Claude Osteen offering off the left-field fence for a double for the Mets in a game won by the Dodgers, 5–2. Joe Ferguson's grand slam in the ninth inning wiped out a 2–1 Mets lead. Troubled by a sore right knee, Mays was able to play in only five games at Al Lang in what would be his final spring. And while he had only 13 at bats on the waterfront, he hit 3 home runs: March 18 off Cincinnati's Pedro Bourbon; March 21 off New York's Fritz Peterson; and March 26 off Atlanta's Jimmy Freeman. Mays retired almost exactly six months later, on September 18, 1973.

March 27, 1975
Ted Simmons (HOF 2020) hit 3 home runs for the Cardinals in a 14–9 loss. The game featured an experimental baseball featuring 96 stitches on its cover, compared to the regulation 108. The game was an offensive explosion, with 6 home runs and 29 hits, including 18 by the Mets.

April 2, 1975
After seventeen springs, Bob Gibson pitched his final game at Al Lang and lost it, 2–1, to the Astros, despite working six solid innings. Milt May's 2-run single was the difference. All-time, Gibson pitched in sixty-three games at Al Lang I and II and was 25-15 with 3 saves and a 2.94 ERA (IP-309, ER-101). He went three years without losing a game on the waterfront between 1967 and 1970.

16

AL LANG II

As the St. Petersburg City Council was mulling over a package of improvements for the city in 1973, one item, "remodeling Al Lang Stadium," was at times on the list and at other times not. But in November, City Manager Raymond Harbaugh, in a memorandum to councilmen, recommended that the city build a new baseball stadium at Al Lang Field. He insisted in the *St. Petersburg Times* that a new facility would cost $1.7 million, compared to the $600,000 to $1 million to renovate the existing structure, which at the time was twenty-seven years old. While several city councilmen had suggested that this project could be eliminated from the city's plans, Harbaugh noted that research indicated that professional baseball contributed at least $3 million annually to the city's economy. To keep baseball in the city, he argued, the field must be improved. Almost exactly one month later, on December 5, the city council approved a $15 million package of improvements for the city, including $1.7 million toward a new stadium on the Al Lang site. No taxes would be used for the entire package. The funds would be generated from bonds backed by the city's 10 percent tax on utilities. Work would begin at the conclusion of the 1975 Florida State League season.

The FSL's St. Petersburg Cardinals took that season as far as it could go, winning the league's best-of-five championship series with the Tampa Tarpons, three games to two, on September 8. The Cards prevailed in Game 5 by a 4–2 score on the strength of a 3-run eighth inning. Second baseman Scott Boras, who would go on to become *Forbes* magazine's "Most Powerful

Sports Agent," scored the winning run and went 2-for-3 with an RBI. Boras played two more seasons, never rising above Class AA.

Tarpon's left-hander Marc Bombard, who had thrown a no-hitter against the Cards at Al Lopez Field in Tampa the night before in Game 4, took the loss in relief. On September 28, there was scheduled a final game at the historic park—a Florida Instructional League game between the Cardinals and Orioles—but someone forgot to tell the wrecking crew, which had already removed a portion of the Astroturf. The eighteen-month project was underway as city crews began transporting the equipment, lights, scoreboard and bleachers to nearby Campbell Park (Sixteenth Street and Seventh Avenue South, one mile west of Al Lang), where spring training and FSL games would be played in 1976 while construction on the new stadium continued. A seventeen-day labor dispute between the major league players and owners delayed spring training; as a result, only thirteen spring games were played at Campbell Park.

On January 22, 1976, with the demolition complete, the city held a "home plate implantation ceremony" to commemorate the start of the construction of the new stadium. While the Northeast High School band played "Take Me Out to the Ballgame," Mayor Charles Schuh was asked to place a new home plate in the same spot as the original Al Lang Field pentagon. He did, but mistakenly positioned it backwards, according to the *Times*.

Following baseball's third work stoppage and second lockout, the first spring game was played at Campbell Park on March 24. The surrogate field was a hitter's paradise, with left field only 293 feet away. The Tigers beat the Cardinals, 8–6, in the first game on Jason Thompson's 2-run home run in the top of the ninth, one of 29 homers hit there during the truncated spring season.

The fifteen-month Al Lang Stadium project was completed in February 1977, but not in time to accommodate the annual old-timers game. Tickets for the twenty-five Grapefruit League games went on sale February 21.

Thirty years to the day that Al Lang Field was christened, Al Lang II made its debut. The accolades were many. *The Sporting News* called it "St. Petersburg's new monument to Organized Baseball in appreciation for 62 years of the happiest association." Stan Musial quipped, "It's out of this world."

And this from the *St. Petersburg Times*: "The rebuilt Al Lang stadium is a gorgeous triumph of modern architecture, a gleaming network of concrete and steel. Surely it is the Taj Mahal of the Grapefruit League this pitch-catch palace."

Al Lang, circa 2006. *Courtesy of Skip Milos.*

Comfortable stadium seats with armrests for the fans, air-conditioned clubhouses for the players and a new quarter diamond behind the center-field fence for infield practice to the delight of the coaches were among the state-of-the-art features. Bermuda grass replaced the artificial-turf infield, a win for the medical trainers. Safety features were added in December 1978 when nets were suspended over the stands behind home plate. And two months later, drains were installed behind home plate to eliminate the rainwater that flowed down through the stands and collected on the field.

Like its predecessors, Al Lang II was a pitchers' park, with dimensions reading 330 feet down the lines in left and right, 365 to both alleys and 400 to center.

All fifty living members of the Hall of Fame were invited. Twenty came to join in the pregame festivities. Renowned trumpeter, bandleader, actor and Cardinals fan Harry James performed the National Anthem.

In the first game, the Mets beat the Cardinals, 10–0, before 7,729. Tom Seaver started and worked three near-perfect innings for the win. Mets right fielder Mike Vail hit the first home run, a 2-run bomb in the fourth inning. The Cards were held to 4 hits.

A year later, the National Association of Professional Baseball Leagues (NAPBL), or Minor League Baseball, moved its offices from the St. Petersburg Chamber of Commerce building into the former detached clubhouse at Al Lang, which was renovated and turned into an office space. The NAPBL had moved from Columbus, Ohio, to St. Petersburg in September 1973. At that time, the honorable sportswriter Bob Broeg wrote:

> *The capital of baseball is not New York or Boston or Detroit or Chicago or St. Louis or Cincinnati or Los Angeles, or any other major league community associated with large crowds and considerable interest. It's not even Cooperstown, New York, the lovely village that is the repository of the Hall of Fame and the game's memory. Baseball's heart beats loudest throughout the year—winter, summer, spring or fall—down here in Florida, particularly in St. Petersburg. And that's why* [NAPBL president] *Henry J. Peters moved the minor league offices here.*

• • • •

March 18, 1978
Reggie Jackson homered and Mickey Rivers led the Yankees with 3 singles and 2 RBIs in a 6–2 win over the Mets in front of 6,819.

March 26, 1980
Future Hall of Fame third baseman Mike Schmidt hit 2 home runs and drove in 6 to lead the Phillies past the Mets, 9–8.

March 23, 1982
Four inches of untreated water backed up in the Al Lang showers, clubhouses and dugout floor ninety minutes before game time. Players from the Royals were forced to shower at North Shore Pool after they lost to the Cardinals, 6–3. Players on both teams sat on metal chairs outside the dugouts.

March 19, 1983
In the season he would become baseball's all-time strikeout king, Nolan Ryan struck out 4 in five innings in a 3–1 Astros loss to the Cardinals.

March 22, 1983
Tom Seaver threw seven shutout innings to beat Boston and Mark "The Bird" Fidrych, who was trying to recapture the glory of his 1976 Rookie of the Year season.

March 12, 1984
White Sox manager and Tampa native Tony LaRussa called for
a bunt with a runner on third with the score tied and two outs in
the top of ninth inning. It worked, as the Sox nipped the Cards,
4–3. The hosts were one out away from a win when pitcher Terry
Clarke dropped a throw at first base for what should have been the
final out of the game. Mike Sodders tripled home the tying run,
and journeyman Dave Stegman dropped a perfect bunt down the
third-base line for a game-winning single. Harold Baines (HOF
2019) hit a home run in the seventh for the White Sox.

March 18, 1984
Tampa's Dwight Gooden, the Mets' nineteen-year-old rookie
sensation, made his Al Lang debut and worked four strong innings,
allowing 1 run, but New York lost to the Blue Jays, 6–3. Another
Tampa native, twenty-year-old Fred McGriff, stroked 2 hits and
scored 2 runs. Gooden, a nonroster invite, pitched his way into the
rotation. He finished the season with a 17-9 record and was named
National League Rookie of the Year.

March 22, 1984
In his first game as a major leaguer at Al Lang, Cal Ripken hit a
four-hundred-foot home run off Bob Forsch as the Orioles defeated
the Cardinals, 2–1.

July 10, 1986
In his only appearance on the waterfront, Randy Johnson (HOF
2015) pitched five innings for the Florida State League West Palm
Beach Expos and left with a 6–3 lead over the St. Pete Cardinals.
The Expos' bullpen failed, however, and the eventual FSL
champion Cardinals won, 7–6, on Jim Fregosi Jr.'s walk-off home
run. Johnson, however, did something he never did in his twenty-
two-year major league career, which included twelve years in the
National League: he scored 2 runs in a game.

17

PARADISE LOST

The word began to spread in the fall of 1985 that the Mets were leaving St. Petersburg for Port St. Lucie, located across the state on the Atlantic coast. City council member and baseball ambassador Bob Stewart and City Manager Bob Obering flew to New York the following February with hopes of persuading owner Nelson Doubleday to stay, but their efforts weren't enough. Stewart was quoted in the *St. Petersburg Times* as saying that Doubleday told them: "There was nothing that we could have done that we didn't do. I said, 'Is there anything we can do to entice you to stay in St. Petersburg?' He said, 'It's not a level playing field. The ball is really out of your court.'"

Doubleday finally made it official the following June 4, when he confirmed that the Mets had signed a fifteen-year lease plus an option with Port St. Lucie. The arrangement would keep the Mets in their new spring home from 1988 through 2002 and called for a $6 million complex with a five-thousand-seat stadium and eight practice fields on a one-hundred-acre site. The Mets would be leaving the only spring home they had ever known, and it would not cost them a penny.

Meanwhile, St. Petersburg city officials estimated the loss of revenue to the city at about $5 million per year. Concerned about the future of baseball in St. Petersburg, voters quickly approved a proposal for a long-term lease with the Cardinals that November.

The headline in the *New York Times* was "Mets Exodus Puzzles Many." Wrote the *Times*'s Joe Durso: "St. Petersburg is a tourist mecca and the center of a bustling spring training area. It is easy to reach through the

Tampa Airport and it is easy to schedule exhibition games within a short radius. Some of the Mets players have bought homes in the area and spend their winters there. So why would the Mets leave all this?" Mets broadcaster Bob Murphy said, "I think practically anyone you to speak to kind of dreads the move because St. Petersburg is such a marvelous place to train."

"I don't know if it is revisionist romanticism but I loved Al Lang field," former Mets pitcher Ron Darling told me recently. "So many memories. I remember the baritone vendor [Tommy Walton], I loved hanging out with George Thorogood [the rocker made an annual trip to Lang to see his beloved Mets], and I think one of the best burgers I ever had was at El Cap [on Fourth Street in St. Pete]. I also found it ironic that the Mets trained at Huggins-Stengel, where those great Yankee teams trained."

But there was more to the story. Not up for debate was the progressive decline in the conditions and spotty maintenance of the Mets' training facilities at the Payson Complex and Huggins-Stengel Field as well as at Al Lang, issues first raised by Councilman Stewart, who was keenly aware of the competition growing among Florida cities for spring training baseball. "The city must be comfortable that we are doing everything we can to keep major league baseball in St. Petersburg in the spring time," Stewart was quoted in the *St. Petersburg Times*.

But it was too late. Despite all of the trappings of the city, it was the decline in the facilities, coupled with the surplus of other suitors, that led to the Mets' departure.

Doubleday took the high road: "As much as we regret leaving St. Petersburg and the fine people we have worked with there, the St. Lucie option was so attractive that we just could not pass it up." Doubleday, whose Palm Beach estate was much closer to the Mets' new home than their old one, became the second New York baseball owner to move his team's spring home closer to his own.

"In the end," longtime Mets public relations director Jay Horwitz told me, "it came down to us getting our own facility."

As a result of the move, 1988 would find St. Pete without two teams and the coveted New York media for the first since 1924, excluding the three years missed due to World War II.

On April 4, 1987, a crowd of 6,477 watched the Mets' final game, including 1,000 Pinellas County students, who were guests of IBM. The team graciously donated their share of the gate—$12,760—to All Children's Hospital. As the *St. Petersburg Times* noted, "There were no brass bands, only faint chalk lines still visible from a band competition held a few days earlier."

The Mets went out the same way they came in, with a loss to St. Louis. The win gave the Cardinals a three-game sweep of the season series (not including a 6–6 tie) and their first Grapefruit League title since 1966. The Cards stole 5 bases off future Hall of Famer Gary Carter, including 2 by shortstop Ozzie Smith, another legend bound for Cooperstown. Singing vendor Tommy Walton, who had been hawking hot dogs and programs at Al Lang for some fifteen years, said he would travel across the state to work some games in Port St. Lucie but would also continue to sing his way through the stands in St. Pete as well.

It was the 107th meeting at Al Lang between the two teams and would effectively end an intense rivalry among the city's two tenants. The Cards held a 58-45-4 edge in the series. "You could feel the tension between the two teams even in spring training," said Magrane. "Especially because the Cardinals beat them out in '85, they beat the Cardinals in '86 to go to the World Series and we beat them out in '87 in the last week. They had all the swagger and the attitude." Magrane admitted there was no love lost between the two. "That's why everybody showed up. And strangely enough, we were sharing Al Lang for all that time."

Prior to the Mets' last Opening Day there on March 7, a 5–1 Cardinals win, Doubleday was presented with a plaque commemorating the team's twenty-six years in St. Petersburg. A crowd of 5,772 tolerated miserable weather. "We will miss you all," Doubleday told the assembly. "We will play the Cardinals over here as many times as we can." The two teams would meet exactly two more times at Al Lang before the Cards moved to Jupiter ten years later.

• • • •

March 14, 1987

On a sunny Saturday afternoon at Al Lang with 6,623 fans watching, including Commissioner Peter Ueberroth and National League president A. Bartlett Giamatti, the Red Sox beat the Mets in a World Series rematch. "Probably most of the fans that are in the stands today weren't able to be at the Series," Mets second baseman Wally Backman told the *St. Petersburg Times*. "To them, it's their own little Series. It did bring back memories when we got off the bus and saw the Red Sox here." Boston starter Al Nipper, who pitched four scoreless innings to get the win, hit Darryl Strawberry in the back with a pitch in the second inning, and the benches cleared. The last time the two faced each other, Strawberry hit a home run to give the Mets an insurance run in their World Series–clinching victory. Nipper was subsequently fined by the commissioner's office for hitting Strawberry.

March 19, 1987
Just before the start of the Mets–White Sox game, a forty-six-year-old St. Petersburg man suffered a heart attack in his seat just behind the Mets' dugout. Several Mets players, including Darryl Strawberry and Gary Carter, helped carry the man to a Bayflight medical helicopter that had landed on the infield after he first received emergency treatment from two nurses who were seated nearby. The start of the game was delayed thirty minutes. Mookie Wilson's home run in the eighth inning broke a 1–1 tie in the Mets' 3–1 win.

March 17, 1988
Forty-one-year-old Nolan Ryan, who came into the game as baseball's all-time strikeout leader, threw to twenty-two-year-old rookie catcher Craig Biggio, both headed for the Hall of Fame. Ryan worked four innings and allowed 8 hits and 5 runs in an 8–7 loss to the Cardinals. He also walked four.

March 21, 1988
Bo Jackson tripled and added 2 singles as the Royals beat the Cardinals, 5–3. George Brett was ejected for throwing his bat after a strikeout.

March 31, 1989
The Cardinals drew 6,598 for their season finale, a 7–0 win over the Phillies. As a result, St. Louis broke its all-time season attendance mark. The Cards drew 78,712 to Al Lang, eclipsing the old mark of 74,981 set in 1988. At one point, the team celebrated eight straight home games with crowds of 6,000 or more, a franchise first. Exactly five months later, the Cardinals' Florida State League team would also set its all-time home attendance mark.

August 31, 1989
On a Fan Appreciation Night doubleheader with the Charlotte Rangers, the St. Petersburg Cardinals became the first team in

Florida State League history to reach two hundred thousand in home attendance and just the seventh Class A team to reach that mark.

November 3, 1989

The Senior Professional Baseball Association made its St. Petersburg debut at Al Lang. The St. Petersburg Pelicans defeated the Orlando Juice, 8–1, in front of 4,017. Its final game at Al Lang came one year, one month and sixteen days later, on December 19, 1990, when the Pelicans edged the Fort Myers Sun Sox, 3–2, on Steve Henderson's walk-off single in the ninth inning before 671 dedicated fans. On December 26, the SPBA was forced to fold after a season and a half.

March 28, 1990

Ten days after Major League Baseball's third lockout and seventh work stoppage ended, the Cardinals hosted the Tigers in the first game at Al Lang. Detroit's Cecil Fielder hit 3 home runs and drove in 6 runs in a 7–3 Tigers win in front of 6,549. Stan Musial threw out the ceremonial first pitch.

July 18, 1991

The nomadic Orioles signed a deal with the City of St. Petersburg and became the sixth of seven teams to call the waterfront their spring training home. The deal with the city was for one year with an option to return if their proposed spring training complex in Naples wasn't completed. It wasn't, and the O's stayed for four more years (but played no games there in 1995 due to the players' strike and their insistence on not filling a team with replacement players).

March 28, 1992

Rookie Pat Mahomes led Minnesota to victory while pitching five scoreless innings in a 2–1, ten-inning win over the Cardinals. No, not Patrick Mahomes, Pat Mahomes, the father of the Kansas City Chiefs' quarterback who had a lifetime record of 42-39 in parts of eleven seasons with the Twins, Mets, Rangers, Cubs, Pirates and Red Sox.

March 7, 1993
Reverend Jesse Jackson watched from the second row as the Cardinals blanked the Orioles, 3–0, on 6 hits. Jackson had been critical of the lack of minorities in baseball front offices and in high-profile positions and had threatened to organize selective fan boycotts. He told the media gathered at Al Lang that day that he planned to talk to players and team officials about the issue. "I think the All-American game should be open to all Americans," was his quote in the *St. Petersburg Times*.

March 16, 1994
Jeff Bagwell (HOF 2017) recorded a home run and 3 RBIs, and Craig Biggio (HOF 2015) added an RBI double and scored 2 runs to lead the Astros past the Cardinals, 7–6. Ozzie Smith (HOF 2002) had a double and a single for the Cards.

March 23, 1996
Bret Boone hit a home run in the Reds' 10–8 loss to the Cardinals, representing the third generation of Boones to drive in a run on the waterfront. It started with his grandfather Ray Boone, who had an RBI single for the Tigers in a 5–3 win over the Yankees on March 16, 1954. It continued with Bret's father, Bob, who delivered a two-out, 3-run single in the Phillies' 15–3 victory over the Cardinals on March 30, 1981. For good measure, Bret's brother Aaron homered for the Reds in a 4–3 win over Tampa Bay in 1998.

March 25, 1996
It was Derek Jeter's (HOF 2020) first game in a big league uniform at Al Lang and Ozzie Smith's last. Jeter managed 1 of only 3 Yankees hits in a 2–0 loss to the Cardinals. Ozzie went 1-for-4. Alan Benes pitched five innings of 1-hit ball to get the win.

August 16, 1996
Starting on October 1, Al Lang will be smoke-free, so say St. Petersburg city officials.

18

THE LAST PASS OF THE BAT(ON)

On May 7, 1996, the pro sports team that to this day still has the longest affiliation with Tampa–St. Petersburg announced it was leaving. With much angst, the St. Louis Cardinals signed a letter of intent to move their spring training operation from St. Petersburg across the state to Jupiter after the 1997 Grapefruit League season. The major league Devil Rays would take over Al Lang in 1998, becoming the seventh team to train on the waterfront and the first team since World War II to train in their home city. "We literally agonized over the decision," Cards co-owner Fred Hauser told Marc Topkin of the *St. Petersburg Times*. "We didn't do it lightly and we didn't do it without feeling." City Administrator Rick Dodge concurred: "I think it's a bittersweet day. There is some sadness in this. At the same time, it was probably a very sensible business decision for them and fortuitously they were able to do it in a way that allowed the Devil Rays to come....There is a real sense of sadness, but there is a joy mixed in with that."

The Cardinals played more than six hundred games on the waterfront parks, and twenty-eight Hall of Famers wore the Cardinals' iconic uniform there, including manager Whitey Herzog, who said of St. Pete:

> *I loved it there. I was there so much with the Yankees* [as a player], *with the Mets* [as a coach and farm director] *and with the Cardinals* [managing for eleven seasons], *it was like my second home. When I first went there in 1955, we stayed at the Soreno Hotel. There weren't any high-rises and we'd just sit on the green benches on the Main Street. And if you saw a woman under 50 you went crazy.*

The team's first managing general partner, Vince Naimoli, saw to it that the Tampa Bay franchise would be the first team in more than fifty years to conduct spring training at home. *Courtesy of Skip Milos.*

The news would also mean the departure of George Kissell, who first went to Waterfront Park in the spring of 1946 and spent at least a portion of each of the next fifty years there with St. Louis as a scout, instructor, coordinator, coach and minor league manager. He is still considered by many to have been the most important person to ever wear the team's uniform. Lou Brock once said of Kissell, "He is the gatekeeper of the Cardinals tradition and the reason the Cardinals play the game right."

In his book *Chasing the Dream*, Hall of Famer Joe Torre called Kissell "the best teacher I ever had." Torre, who was on the waterfront for twelve springs with St. Louis either as a player or a manager, was converted from catcher to third baseman by Kissell in the spring of 1971, Torre's best season. The *St. Petersburg Times* described one of their training sessions this way: "Kissell walked Torre into the outfield at Al Lang Field and told him to stand eight feet from the outfield wall facing it. Then Kissell stood behind him and threw baseballs at the wall. Torre had to react as the balls ricocheted back at him just as a third baseman would do when one is whacked his way."

Twenty springs later, it was the ever-present Kissell who helped Torre develop a liberating managing style that would serve him well during his historic twelve-year run as manager of the Yankees. Torre was in his first year of managing the Cardinals, and Kissell was the team's spring training coordinator. "He held a yellow pad during the games and jotted down things about our club that needed attention," wrote Torre. "He had a favorite line: 'Joe, who wrote the book?' And I'd say, 'Nobody wrote the book, George.' That was his way of reminding me that I could make any move I wanted as a manager as long as I had the right reasons for it—whether it was unpopular or unorthodox."

Kissell died in 2008, ironically, Al Lang's last year as a spring training site. His memorial service was held on the same infield that had served as his classroom. Many of the more than two hundred mourners present were former students of the man they called "The Professor."

"That stadium held all kinds of memories for so many of us," Magrane told me. "I have always considered myself a lover of the history of the game, because I fell in love with it so early. Back in that time, all these former Cardinals were sitting in the stands watching the games.

> *You would see Gibby* [Bob Gibson] *and Lou Brock and all of these guys would be at the park. There was such a connection to the tradition with them around. It was all very humbling when they would call you by your first name and you would think, "That guy knows who I am?" You would pass them and in the hallway with "Hello, Mr. Musial," and it would be, "Hey, Joe good to see you." It was like we're in some place kinda serious. Don't mess this up.*
>
> *You would think, "Well, I guess if they like me, it will be alright." You're not with the Cleveland Indians or whatever. You were really part of something very special, and it created that mindset that you did not want to drop the baton or disappoint. It really brought you up a few notches. There is no cruising through this. Seeing that jersey with the birds on the bat. It was inspiring.*

Other changes were coming. The St. Petersburg City Council soon voted, 7–0, to approve a new name for the stadium, Florida Power Park: Home of Al Lang Field. In 2003, it was changed again to Progress Energy Park at Al Lang Field.

Even the tourists were changing. The number of seasonal visitors in Pinellas County had steadily increased over the years, but 1999 was the first year on record in which summer visitors outnumbered winter visitors, according to a story in the *St. Petersburg Times* on February 10, 2000.

Pablo Ortega throws the first pitch in Tampa Bay Devil Rays history in a Gulf Coast League game against the Yankees. Tampa Bay Times *photo.*

Pablo Ortega wasn't a tourist, but he, too, was new to St. Pete. A native of Nueva Laredo, Mexico, the nineteen-year-old Devil Rays prospect hadn't thrown a pitch yet and had already soaked through his multicolor home uniform on a scorching morning in late June as the clock ticked toward noon. It was a typical day in the life of the Gulf Coast League (GCL), a developmental league and the lowest rung on baseball's ladder. But on this day, the midday humidity was the only thing that was normal for a GCL game. There were people standing in line to get through the gates at Al Lang long before the first pitch. There were school buses of children from their summer day camps filling the parking lot. A commemorative game ticket, program and scorecard. Concessions. Live television and radio. All for one game in a league with a normal daily attendance of zero.

It was the first game in the history of the Tampa Bay Devil Rays organization, on June 19, 1996, between the brand-spanking-new Devil Rays and youngsters from the ninety-three-year-old Yankees franchise. "It was a minor league game," said city rep Dodge, "but a major league day." Cuban refugee Alex Sanchez got the first hit. The Rays' leadoff man dropped a bunt single up the third-base line on the first pitch he saw. Sanchez and pitcher Victor Zambrano and the Yankees designated hitter Nick Johnson and shortstop Cristian Guzman were the only players from

Rays mascot "Raymond" works the crowd at Al Lang. *Courtesy of Skip Milos.*

the game who would play in big leagues. The Yankees embarrassed the young D-Rays, 10–1.

The crowd of 7,582 was not only an unofficial league record, but also, who would have ever imagined it would be the Devil Rays / Rays organization's largest crowd ever at Al Lang? That's right, bigger than any crowd to see the major league team. Two years later, in the Devil Rays' first major league spring camp, attendance was already an issue, as so-so crowds watched the inaugural team. "I'm not sure what to make of it," Managing General Partner Vince Naimoli told the *St. Petersburg Times*. It was a sentiment that would be repeated over and over again among Tampa Bay's baseball fans.

• • • •

March 20, 1997

The last game between the Yankees and Cardinals on the waterfront saw St. Louis beat up Tampa native Dwight Gooden, 8–3, in front of 5,782 fans. The contest featured two future Hall of Fame managers: Joe Torre and Tony LaRussa. It was also the 138th game played between these two teams in St. Petersburg's three waterfront parks. The Cardinals won the series, 77-60-1, claiming 17 of the last 21 games beginning in 1960. The final game was eight days shy of being exactly seventy years after the waterfront's first battle between the two teams, which was also the first matchup of defending league champions.

March 25, 1997

The Cardinals played their last game on the waterfront after fifty-seven years. A crowd of 6,616, including Cardinal Hall of Famers Stan Musial, Bob Gibson, Red Schoendienst and Lou Brock, was on hand for the festive night, which included an unusual first pitch: Cardinals owner William DeWitt to Devil Rays owner Vince Naimoli. Musial played "Take Me Out to the Ballgame" on his harmonica. The players wore shoulder patches that read "Thank you St. Petersburg, 1937–97." There was even one last rain delay and one last Cardinals win, 6–3, over the Phillies.

February 26, 1998

The expansion major league Devil Rays beat Florida State University, 6–3, at Al Lang in their first exhibition game before

4,672 fans. The Rays went five straight innings without a hit and trailed, 3–1, before busting out for 5 runs in the eighth. Kevin Cash, who would become the manager of the Rays in 2015, batted third and played first base for the Seminoles. He was hitless in two at bats.

February 27, 1998
Tampa Bay played its first game against a major league opponent and lost, 2–1, to the defending world champion Marlins. Bubba Trammell's home run to left field in the third inning was the first in team history. Morning showers kept the crowd down to 4,918. Eight-year-old Thea Cabreros sang the anthem, and the team honored the late Tommy Walton, the legendary singing vendor.

March 2, 1998
Second baseman Miguel Cairo made several stellar defensive plays and was 2-for-4 with an RBI, and the Devil Rays scored 5 unearned runs in a 6–2 win over the Royals, their first victory over a major league opponent. Only 2,880 were on the waterfront to witness it.

August 24, 2000
In his fifth rehab start after suffering a fractured left humerus in a start against Texas at Tropicana Field on May 26, 1999, Tony Saunders unbelievably suffered the same injury on the same arm again. The injury occurred in the third inning of his Florida State League start against the Clearwater Phillies. Within a minute, a hard rain began to fall as players from both teams held the mound tarp over Saunders as he lay on the mound writhing in pain while waiting for an ambulance to take him to nearby Bayfront Hospital. The injury ended the twenty-six-year-old's career.

August 28, 2000
The last minor league game was played at Florida Power Park, Home of Al Lang Field, as the St. Petersburg Devil Rays beat the Vero Beach Dodgers, 12–7, in an FSL game that saw 9 errors.

March 2, 2002
Jim Morris and Dennis Quaid threw out the ceremonial first pitches at the home opener before the Rays-Braves game to

promote the release of the movie *The Rookie*. Hall of Famer Greg Maddux started for the Braves. The crowd of 5,032 saw the Braves win, 3–2.

March 20, 2002
Baseball's all-time leader in runs scored and stolen bases, Rickey Henderson, didn't steal a base or score a run in his only game at Al Lang, but he did get 2 hits and an RBI in the Boston's 4–1 win. It was his last spring training.

March 18, 2005
In a night game against his former team, twelve-time All-Star Roberto Alomar made 2 errors in one inning, struck out and pulled himself out of the Devil Rays lineup in their 5–4 loss to the Blue Jays. The next morning, in a press conference in the owner's suite at Progress Energy Park, the thirty-seven-year-old future Hall of Famer announced his retirement.

March 12, 2008
Fight! In what many believed was a galvanizing moment for the 2008 American League champion Rays, Al Lang hosted its last dustup. Trying to stretch a single, Yankees infielder Shelley Duncan slid with spikes up and gashed the right leg of Rays second baseman Akinori Iwamura. Benches cleared, and Rays right fielder Jonny Gomes, Duncan and Yankees coaches Kevin Long and Bobby Meacham were ejected from the game. Five days earlier in Tampa, Rays infielder Elliot Johnson crashed into New York's Francisco Cervelli in a home-plate collision, fracturing the catcher's wrist. Gomes and five members of the Yankees were disciplined by Major League Baseball. Duncan and Melky Cabrera were suspended three games each and fined. Manager Joe Girardi, Meacham and Long were also fined. The Rays got a 7–6 win.

March 28, 2008
The last Grapefruit League game was played at Al Lang. A crowd of 6,759—the largest there for a Rays game and 4 more than the crowd that attended the Rays-Tigers game twelve days earlier—was on hand as the Rays fell to the Reds, 6–3, bringing their all-time record there to 72-70-5. Al Lang's closest living relatives—great-

nephews John and Hugh Fagen—threw out the ceremonial first pitches. Hall of Famer Monte Irvin, who played at Al Lang Field in 1951 as a member of the New York Giants, signed autographs for the fans. The Reds' Adam Dunn hit the last home run, and left-hander Danny Herrera, who would not record any saves in his four-year major league career, earned the save and thus threw the last pitch.

• • • •

MEMBERS OF THE RAYS' front office voted on an all-time team made up of players who suited up for home games on the waterfront:

C   Yogi Berra, Gary Carter
1B   Lou Gehrig, Stan Musial
2B   Rogers Hornsby, Red Schoendienst
SS   Cal Ripken, Ozzie Smith
3B   Wade Boggs, Ken Boyer
OF   Joe DiMaggio, Willie Mays, Monte Irvin, Mickey Mantle, Lou Brock, Babe Ruth, Darryl Strawberry
P   Bob Gibson, Tom Seaver, Nolan Ryan, Whitey Ford, Steve Carlton, Dennis Eckersley, Lee Smith

EPILOGUE

Walk up to Al Lang Stadium today, and you will experience none of the feelings of civic pride that should emanate from such a baseball landmark. Lang's name isn't even featured on the ballpark's exterior. There are more than four thousand historical markers in Florida. Al Lang's grounds haven't merited one.

When Al Lang II was completed in 1977, seventeen years after Lang's death, city officials dedicated a twelve-by-eighteen-inch bronze plaque in his memory. It remains inconspicuously there now on a small pedestal outside the park, next to a green and yellow plastic newspaper box filled with free tourist guides. A publication for tourists! Oh, how Al Lang would have loved the irony. That tiny plaque holding forty-nine words is the only visible tribute to the man who did more for baseball in Florida than anyone else. Al's legacy in forty-nine words. Roughly two tweets for a man the *St. Petersburg Evening Independent* ranked behind only the city's founder, General John C. Williams, as its most important historical figure.

In 1998, St. Petersburg Chamber of Commerce officials unveiled eighty-five brass home plates, known as the Baseball Boulevard, to be installed across the city from Al Lang Stadium to Tropicana Field. Each plate featured a significant event meant to celebrate the city's baseball history; some included Lang's name. Sadly, the home plates have, for the most part, disappeared.

After the final Grapefruit League game at the ballpark, historian Will Michaels wrote in the *St. Petersburg Times*, "Whatever the future may hold for the stadium, the city owes it to Al [Lang] to continue to commemorate his name and memory in some prominent manner."

It is both disappointing and puzzling. Especially so when considering what other nearby municipalities have done to memorialize their baseball histories. The Tinker Field History Plaza in Orlando and Clearwater's Monument Park at Jack Russell Stadium are magnificent, educational and reverent. While those cities have rich baseball histories, neither reached the level of St. Pete.

Over much of nine decades, it would be difficult to deny that St. Pete's ballparks were the city's signature piece, a source of pride for residents and local businesses and at the center of the city's largest industry: tourism. As a gathering place, it has been there when the city has called. A multi-use facility? It may have been the first. The site has hosted an eclectic list of events: religious revivals, band competitions, playing-card tournaments, pro soccer games, college football contests, women's professional baseball games, fashion shows, horse shows, at least one cricket match, beauty pageants, a beauty school, circuses, concerts, an expansion-draft party, a world championship horseshoe-pitching tournament, World War II militia training, debates, civic dedications, hobby conventions, something called a mutt derby race and the city's annual free Halloween parties for children, which ran from 1948 to 1993. For a while, it hosted the city's famed "Fountain of Youth."

The last games played at the waterfront involving professional baseball came on March 9–16, 2014, as part of the city's annual eight-game International Baseball Series. Babe Ruth's ninety-seven-year-old daughter, Julia Ruth Stevens, came from her home in Las Vegas to throw out the ceremonial first pitch before one of the games between a minor league squad from the Baltimore Orioles and the Canadian National Junior Team. "Daddy loved it here," she told the assemblage.

At the last major league game played there in 2008, a nostalgic baseball fan named Rob Gray enlisted the help of friends to hold up signs that read "We'll drink a cup of kindness yet to days of Al Lang signs."

"It's the end of the world as we know it," he told the *St. Petersburg Times*.

WORKS CITED

Books

Appel, Marty. *Casey Stengel: Baseball's Greatest Character*. New York: Anchor Books, 2017.

Arsenault, Raymond. *St. Petersburg and the Florida Dream*. Gainesville: University Press of Florida, 1999.

Baker, Rick. *Mangroves to Major League*. St. Petersburg, FL: Southern Heritage Press, 2000.

DeYoung, Bill. *Vintage St. Pete: The Golden Age of Tourism*. St. Petersburg, FL: St. Petersburg Press, 2022.

Fountain, Charles. *Under the March Sun*. New York: Oxford University Press, 2009.

Fuller, Walter. *St. Petersburg and Its People*. St. Petersburg, FL: Great Outdoors Publishing, 1972.

Gibson, Bob. *Stranger to the Game*. New York: Penguin, 1994.

Henig, Adam. *Baseball Under Siege*. N.p.: self-published, 2016.

Jacobson, Steve. *Carrying Jackie's Torch: The Players Who Integrated Baseball—And America*. Chicago: Lawrence Hill Books, 2007.

McCarthy, Kevin. *Babe Ruth in Florida*. Conshocken, PA: Infinity Publishing, 2002.

McCarver, Tim, and Phil Pepe. *Few and Chosen*. Chicago: Triumph Books, 2003.

Michaels, Wes. *The Making of St. Petersburg*. Charleston, SC: The History Press, 2012.

Montville, Leigh. *The Big Bam*. New York: Doubleday, 2006.

Mormino, Gary. *Land of Sunshine, State of Dreams: A Social History of Modern Florida*. Gainsville: University Press of Florida, 2008.

Sitler, Nevin. *Warm Wishes from Sunny St. Pete: The Success Story of Promoting the Sunshine City*. Charleston, SC: The History Press, 2014.

Torre, Joe, and Tom Verducci. *Chasing the Dream*. New York: Bantam, 1997.

White, Bill. *Uppity: My Untold Story about the Games People Play*. New York: Grand Central Publishing, 2011.

Zimmer, Don. *A Baseball Life*. New York: Total / Sports Illustrated, 2001.

Articles

Francis, Bill. "Monte Irvin Remembers." Baseball History series. National Baseball Hall of Fame and Museum. Cooperstown, New York.

Keller, Melissa. "Spring Training and Publicity in the Sunshine City." *Tampa Bay History* 15, no. 2 (1993).

Sitler, Nevin. "Selling St. Petersburg: John Lodwick and the Promotion of a Florida Paradise." Master's thesis, University of South Florida, 2006.

Warrington, Robert D. "St. Petersburg: Its Beginnings and the Phillies' Experience in 1915," In *The National Pastime: Baseball in the Sunshine State*, edited by Cecilia Tan. Phoenix, AZ: Society for American Baseball Research, 2016.

Newspapers and News Services

Associated Press
Atlanta Journal-Constitution
Boston Herald
Cincinnati Post
Literary Digest
Minneapolis Star Tribune
New York Daily News
New York Herald Tribune
New York Times
Politico
Scripps Howard

Sport magazine
The Sporting News
St. Petersburg Evening Independent
St. Petersburg Times

ABOUT THE AUTHOR

Rick Vaughn is a veteran in the sports communications field, having served more than thirty years with baseball's Baltimore Orioles and Tampa Bay Rays and the NFL's Washington Redskins. He served as the lead PR executive for the closing of Baltimore's beloved Memorial Stadium and the opening of the iconic Oriole Park at Camden Yards, the launch of the Tampa Bay Devil Rays' expansion franchise and its rebranding to "Rays" in 2008 and traveled to Japan with the 2002 MLB All-Star team and to Cuba with the Rays in 2016. He is presently the executive director of Los Angeles Angels manager Joe Maddon's Respect 90 Foundation. He and his wife, Sue, have been married for forty-two years and are the proud parents of Amanda and Elissa and grandparents of Mason. They reside in Palm Harbor, Florida.

Visit us at
www.historypress.com